P9-DGR-529

Forthcoming Volumes in the New Church's Teaching Series
James E. Griffiss, series editor

Opening the Bible

The New
Church's Teaching Series
Volume 2

Opening
the Bible

Roger Ferlo

COWLEY PUBLICATIONS
Cambridge ✦ *Boston*
Massachusetts

The title *The Church's Teaching Series* is used by permission of the Domestic and Foreign Missionary Society. Use of the series title does not constitute the Society's endorsement of the content of the work.

Published in the United States of America by Cowley Publications, a division of the Society of St. John the Evangelist. No portion of this book may be reproduced, stored in or introduced into a retrieval system, or transmitted, in any form or by any means—including photocopying—without the prior written permission of Cowley Publications, except in the case of brief quotations embodied in critical articles and reviews.

Library of Congress Cataloging-in-Publication Data:
Ferlo, Roger, 1951–
  Opening the Bible / Roger Ferlo.
      p.   cm. — (The new church's teaching series; v. 2)
  Includes bibliographical references.
  ISBN 1-56101-144-4 (alk. paper)
  1. Bible—Study and teaching. I. Title. II. Series.
BS600.2.F45   1997
220.6'1—dc21   97-21735
                                                       CIP

Scripture quotations are from the *New Revised Standard Version* of the Bible, © 1989 by the Division of Christian Education of the National Council of the Churches of Christ in the USA. Used by permission. All rights reserved.

Cynthia Shattuck, editor; Vicki Black, copyeditor and designer
Cover art taken from a gospel book of the Franco-Saxon school, second half of the ninth century.

Royalties from the sale of books in the New Church's Teaching Series have been donated to the *Anglican Theological Review*.

This book is printed on recycled, acid-free paper and was produced in Canada.

Cowley Publications • 28 Temple Place
Boston, Massachusetts 02111
1-800-225-1534 • http://www.cowley.org/~cowley

Table of Contents

Preface

The New Church's Teaching Series

Almost fifty years ago a series called The Church's Teaching was launched with the publication of Robert Dentan's *The Holy Scriptures* in 1949. Again in the 1970s the church commissioned another church's teaching series for the next generation of Anglicans. Originally the series was part of an effort to give the growing postwar churches a sense of Anglican identity: what Anglicans share with the larger Christian community and what makes them distinctive within it. During that seemingly more tranquil era it may have been easier to reach a consensus and to speak authoritatively. Now, at the end of the twentieth century, consensus and authority are more difficult; there is considerably more diversity of belief and practice within the churches today, and more people than ever who have never been introduced to the church at all.

The books in this new teaching series attempt to encourage and respond to the times—and to the challenges that will usher out the old century and bring in the new. This new series differs from the previous two in significant ways: it has no official status, claims no special authority, speaks in a personal voice, and comes not out of committees but from scholars and pastors meeting and talking informally together. It assumes a different readership: adults who are not "cradle Anglicans," but who come from other religious traditions or from no tradition at all, and who want to know what Anglicanism has to offer.

As the series editor I want to thank E. Allen Kelley, former president of Morehouse Publishing, for initially inviting me to bring together a group of teachers and pastors who could write with learning and conviction about their faith. I am grateful both to him and to Morehouse for participating in the early development of the series.

Since those initial conversations there have been substantial changes in the series itself, but its basic purpose has remained: to explore the themes of the Christian life through Holy Scripture, historical and contemporary theology, worship, spirituality, and social witness. It is our hope that all readers, Anglicans and otherwise, will find the books an aid in their continuing growth into Christ.

James E. Griffiss
Series Editor

Acknowledgments

Over the years, many communities have welcomed me as pastor, teacher, and friend. This book is their book. They have taught me more about reading the Bible than I could ever teach them.

My thanks go to the parishioners at the Church of the Good Shepherd, Augusta, Georgia, and to the sisters of the Order of St. Helena, who first heard me try out the ideas in this book.

At the Church of the Redeemer in Pittsburgh, my parishioners' tremendous thirst to learn was matched only by the generous patience with which they greeted what I had to say.

Pamela Foster invited me to teach about the Bible in the diaconal training program in the Diocese of Pittsburgh. Although my students and I were often poles apart theologically, they showed me how reading the Bible with open minds and lowered voices could unite us more than our theological differences would divide us. Also during that time, my colleagues in the Jewish-Christian Dialogue of Pittsburgh introduced me to the joys and challenges of interfaith readings of the Bible.

Most recently, as rector of the Church of St. Luke in the Fields and chaplain of St. Luke's School in New York City, I have been privileged to lead the Monday night Rector's Bible Study week after week. The members of the group graciously agreed to read the book in manuscript, and it has profited much from their comments. I am also grateful to Daniel Ade, Alvin Hart, Rob Snyder, and Janet Malcolm for advice at strategic moments, and to Michael Feria and Gary Gura for help in preparing the manuscript at an early stage.

As an independent scholar, I could not have written this book without the vast resources of the Research Division of the New York Public Library, offered so freely and generously to all who seek to use them. Thanks are also due to the staffs of both the Pierpont Morgan Library and the St. Mark's Library of the General Theological Seminary in New York City, for several kindnesses.

In addition to my Monday night class, a number of people have taken the time to read this manuscript in its various drafts. I am grateful to my fellow writers in this series, some of whom gathered in Evanston to hash out our preliminary ideas, and especially to James Griffiss and Michael Johnston. I am deeply indebted to my friend, parishioner, and former teacher, Professor Richard Corney of the General Seminary, for his meticulous reading of the entire manuscript at a crucial stage, and for the numerous times his intervention saved me from committing yet another Old Testament howler. Such teachers and friends are rare. Cynthia Shattuck has been the ideal editor, which means that any remaining errors of fact and judgment are my own responsibility.

My parents, Albert and Nathaline Ferlo, in whose house I learned to read, have supported me in my work through the years with unswerving good humor, patience, and love. My wife Anne Harlan, and my daughter Liz Harlan-Ferlo, both of them gifted writers and demanding readers, have had faith in me and in this project from the start. I owe them more than I know how to say.

Two other people have read this manuscript—Pam Foster and Rodgers Wood. For several years, they joined me for a weekly clergy "Bible study" at a neighborhood tavern in Millvale, just outside Pittsburgh. As the reader will soon see, there is ample Reformation precedent for debating Scripture in alehouses. Even though we consistently forgot to bring our Bibles with us, those weekly sessions at Grant's taught me what I know about conversation, loyalty, and friendship.

Arthur McNulty organized our Bible study, but did not live to read this book. His sudden loss to us is incalculable. *Opening the Bible* is dedicated to his memory.

Chapter 1

Why Read the Bible?

A few years ago a parishioner generously offered to buy a set of Bibles to place in the pews of our church in Greenwich Village. Many parishioners liked the convenience of having Bibles handy (and a few, I suspect, never noticed the difference), but their presence also made a surprising number of people uneasy. They had come to the Episcopal Church to get away from the fundamentalist Christianity of their childhood, and Bibles in the pews reminded them too vividly of the revival tent. There was even speculation—only half in jest—that the new rector harbored a secret fundamentalist agenda (this was Greenwich Village, after all). But the most telling comment came from a lifelong Episcopalian and much-beloved retired priest, who looked at me long and hard and told me what his own mother had taught him years before in West Texas: "Son, to read the Bible in church, all you ever needed was a Prayer Book."

Slide into a pew in any Episcopal church and you will almost always find copies of the *Book of Common Prayer* and *The Hymnal 1982*. Bibles, though, are scarce. Even if you should find one in church, you would almost never be called upon to use it. Bible-reading lies at the heart of Anglican history and Anglican worship, and yet in most Episcopal churches Bibles are not much in evidence.

History would lead you to expect otherwise. The English Reformation began, after all, with a ringing endorsement of every believer's right to read the Bible freely and openly, translated into a language everyone could understand. Rejecting Roman tradition and papal authority, the early reformers insisted that in matters of faith only the Bible mattered. Holy Scripture, it is written in the Articles of Religion, a founding document of Anglican belief, "containeth all things necessary to salvation....whatsoever is not read therein, nor may be proved thereby, is not required of any man."[1]

The reformed English church became a Bible-reading church. Thomas Cranmer saw to that. As the first archbishop of the Church of England (of which the American Episcopal Church is a direct descendant), Cranmer substantially increased the amount of Scripture to be read aloud during public worship. In the course of just one year almost the entire body of sacred writings would be proclaimed in parish churches, not in Latin but in English, "that the people (by daily hearing of holy Scripture read in the Church) should continually profit more and more in the knowledge of God, and be the more inflamed with the love of his true religion" (BCP 866).

Cranmer's prayer book is drenched in the language of the Bible. So are its successors, including the 1979 *Book of Common Prayer* that Episcopalians use today. No wonder my Texan friend insisted that you didn't need a Bible in the pew; almost every phrase in the *Book of Common Prayer* seems to quote or paraphrase it. The prayer book he grew up with, published in 1928, printed two New Testament readings for every Sunday of the year, but the range of readings for Sunday has expanded considerably since 1928 and there are now too many to print in the prayer book itself. Even so, like almost all its predecessors, it does provide one book of the Bible in its entirety—the book of Psalms, known as the Psalter. The Psalter is the cornerstone of our common prayer. To say or sing the Psalter is to pray the Bible. Day by day and week by week, we use prayers that Jesus himself probably knew by heart.

Besides the Psalter, other extended sections of Scripture appear in the prayer book as well, among them Mary's song at the annunciation ("My soul doth magnify the Lord"); Simeon's song in the temple as he held the infant Christ ("O Lord, now lettest thou thy servant depart in peace"); excerpts from Isaiah and Revelation; and passages from Paul's letters celebrating Christ as the new Passover ("Christ our Passover is sacrificed for us"). In Cranmer's time and for generations afterwards, the daily repetition of these psalms and canticles in parish churches and private devotions helped shape the everyday language of the English people. By decree of the king, an imposing printed Bible was to be placed in every parish church, open to be seen and read by anyone literate enough to approach it. Even now in many British and North American churches a large Bible or lectionary book can be found open on a lectern carved to resemble an eagle, symbolizing God's saving word soaring above the congregation.

It is one thing to pray the Bible in the words of the prayer book. Anglicans are used to this. But reading the Bible on its own, outside the context of prayer book worship, was never a simple matter—either in Reformation times or in ours. Free access to an English-language Bible provoked storms of controversy in the 1500s and 1600s. Within a hundred years of Cranmer's death at the stake in 1556 during the reign of the Catholic Queen Mary, controversy over how to read the Bible (or rather, how to control its reading) would contribute to the execution of one of Mary's Stuart successors, Charles I, and help to usher all of England into a bloody religious war. Henry VIII himself, whose rejection of papal authority in the matter of his divorce and remarriage set the stage for Cranmer's reforms, was at best ambivalent about giving his subjects much freedom to read the book for themselves. Some of the things the Bible says are not very flattering to absolute monarchs, and Henry knew it.

Resistance in high places to the free and open reading of the Bible remained intense in the decades that followed, and sometimes ended in violence. It was only after Elizabeth came to the throne in 1558 that general access to an English Bible was assured for almost every reader in the kingdom. By the end of her reign, the English-language Bible had taken hold of the religious imagination in Britain, as it would soon thereafter in the American colonies. In the sonorous words of the preface to the Bible translation authorized by Elizabeth's successor, King James I (the famous "King James Version"), the Bible was "a fountain of most pure water springing up into everlasting life. . . . the end and the reward of the study thereof [is] fellowship with the Saints, participation of the heavenly nature, fruition of an inheritance immortal, undefiled, and that shall never fade away."[2]

Both for these first generations of Anglicans and for Anglicans today, the Bible was not meant to be studied in isolation. Reading the Bible, even reading it in solitude, remains a community venture. For Anglicans, an individual's freedom to interpret the Bible, justly celebrated as the birthright of every baptized Christian, has always been subject to the moderating influence of the theologian learned in history, and of the licensed preacher. Worried that the subversive rabble would start expounding Scripture in alehouses, Cranmer instructed Bible readers in 1538 that if they were in doubt as to the meaning of any biblical passage, they were to consult "learned men" who were authorized to expound Scripture's meaning. A generation later, the great Elizabethan theologian Richard Hooker, refuting the Puritans who claimed that the "bare reading" of the Bible would suffice for any Christian, insisted that the book must always be read in context—not just in the context of common worship, but also in the context of received tradition. "Bare reading" of Scripture, he said in a memorable phrase, provided "bare feeding" for hungry souls.[3] The Bible demands a commentary, and reliable, responsible commentary demands expertise. One should not read into the Bible what it cannot say.

Reading the Bible today, we have come a long way from riotous sessions in Elizabethan alehouses. Like Anglicans everywhere, Episcopalians enjoy the freedom to read the Bible anywhere and at any time, and revere it as God's own word to God's own people. But we also inherit Hooker's judicious moderation in interpreting God's word—a moderation grounded in respect for traditions about the Bible shared by the Christian church from its earliest days. We reserve the right to exercise our God-given reason in applying the wisdom of these ancient and often difficult texts to our own lives and to our own experience. For present-day Episcopalians, this faith in Scripture, tradition, and reason guides everything we do when we read the Bible. For us as for Hooker, to read the Bible responsibly, context is paramount:

- the context of public worship in which the Bible has been heard, prayed, and preached;
- the context of ancient cultures and languages in which the Bible first was written and published;

- the context of tradition, especially the first four centuries of Christian believing, when characteristically Christian methods of reading the Bible began to take coherent shape;
- the context of almost two thousand years of intellectual, scientific, religious, and social change, in the midst of which, in diverse times and places, Episcopalians along with other Christians have wrestled with the meaning of the Bible in our lives.

How do Anglicans read the Bible today? Surely not as Archbishop Cranmer and King James I did, or even the way our own grandparents did. We live in a different world, a world of personal computers and interactive CD-ROMS, of hypertexts and high-resolution television, a world where the act of reading itself has been radically transformed in method, style, and intention. Books are treated differently now than they were by people in Cranmer and Hooker's time. They look different and they feel different. Although books are far more readily available than they were four hundred years ago, they no longer wield an intrinsic authority. It can be argued that in our own culture, where books are omnipresent, fewer people read anything at all with the diligence and care that a serious book demands. They often don't have the time; even more often, they don't have the skill. This is as true for the Bible as it is for any other book.

The tremendous technological changes in how and what we read pose compelling questions for contemporary Anglicans as we open our Bibles. In spite of our extraordinary technical sophistication in navigating new forms of both print and electronic media, we have become less biblically literate than our forebears. Do we read the Bible as much as our grandparents or great-grandparents used to read? Do we have the time? Do we even know how? Have we lost touch with our tradition? Or has the tradition lost touch with us? Have we reasoned ourselves away from faith in the Bible? Can we still regard the Bible with the reverence and awe with which our ancestors regarded it—as "the revealed Word of God" and "the rule and ultimate standard of faith," as the *Book of Common Prayer* describes it?

None of these questions can be answered with a simple yes or no. Contemporary attitudes toward the Bible are varied and complicated. Not only have both the church and its prayer book changed dramatically over the centuries, but there has also been an explosion of knowledge about the Bible itself: how it came to be written, how it was published and translated, and how our own culture differs from the cultures that produced it. Shifts in our deeply held certainties—about authority and power, or about matters of race and gender and class, or about the nature of scientific knowledge—determine for us (often without our knowing it) the way we seek for meaning and guidance in these ancient texts.

Within the Episcopal Church there now exists a wide spectrum of approaches to reading the Bible, and an even wider spectrum of convictions about the nature of the book itself. Episcopalians do not always agree with one another about the meaning of specific passages of the Bible, or about the scope of its authority. Reading the Bible in this sometimes highly charged atmosphere is not easy. Episcopalians recognize no central interpreting authority to decide for them what is true and what is not. This dispersal of authority exacts a cost. Many Episcopalians are ignorant of how the Bible works—its history as a sacred book, its characteristic rhetorical strategies, its complex relationship to living traditions of belief, including their own. They have no idea what a responsible method of reading would look like. Worried that they don't know enough *about* the Bible, or that they don't believe hard enough *in* the Bible, many faithful people in the Episcopal Church hesitate to read the Bible on their own at all.

But it can be done. Certainly great differences separate us from the assumptions of our Reformation forebears in reading and interpreting Scripture; even greater differences may separate Episcopalians from one another as they read. Some of those differences will become evident as this book unfolds—differences about the role of women in the church's ministry, for example, or even differences about the meaning of key Christian doctrines like the resurrection of the body and the virgin birth. But in spite of their divisions, Episcopalians as people of faith share a central conviction about the Bible: that God the Holy Spirit lives and breathes in these pages, and in those who seek with humility and compassion to understand such challenging, ancient texts.

Like all books, the Bible has a history that determines how it should be read. It is a history that must be learned, and its boundaries respected. We cannot read into the Bible what was never there. Nor can we simply pick and choose the texts that meet our needs or reinforce our prejudices, wresting passages out of context and turning them into slogans.

But if the Bible has a history, it also recounts a history. It is our history, the history of God's continuing actions among us—a history of God's relationship with humanity in Jesus the Christ that is at once cosmic and intimate, both timeless and immediate. Through our baptism, we claim God's history as our own. As we read the Bible Episcopalians make this claim together, not shying away from controversy or disagreement, always ready to engage both the Bible and one another in passionate conversation, but always seeking a common ground upon which to read and respond to the Spirit of God that breathes through these pages. For all its wonderful and maddening difficulties, its frustrating obscurities and rich complexities, the Bible remains eminently readable. Through its pages God's holy word still speaks powerfully to ordinary readers faithfully reading.

~ Ruminating on the Bible

How does God's word speak to us today? What does it feel like to read a book that is the word of God? Think for a moment about the activity of reading. We say that we read to "escape." We are "absorbed" in a book, or "lost" in it. A book so excites our imagination that we "consume" it, or it consumes us. All these metaphors for reading are so much a part of our everyday language that it is difficult to think of them as metaphors at all. But it was not always so. Try to step back for a moment. What would it feel like to consume the sacred book? Or to be consumed by it? To eat it, to chew it, swallow it, digest it, to make it a part of you? That is exactly what the prophet Jeremiah imagined about the word of God:

> Your words were found, and I ate them,
>   and your words became to me a joy
>   and the delight of my heart;
> for I am called by your name,
>   O LORD, God of hosts. (Jeremiah 15:16)

The impact of this metaphor was not lost on later biblical writers. A younger contemporary of Jeremiah, the prophet Ezekiel, describes a vision of a hand stretched toward him, spreading out a scroll that had writing "on the front and on the back, and written on it were words of lamentation and mourning and woe":

> He said to me, O mortal, eat what is offered to you; eat this scroll, and go, speak to the house of Israel. So I opened my mouth, and he gave me the scroll to eat. He said to me, Mortal, eat this scroll that I give you and fill your stomach with it. Then I ate it; and in my mouth it was as sweet as honey. (Ezekiel 3:1-3)

Centuries later, adapting this passage for his own prophetic purposes, the Christian writer of the book of Revelation will recount the words of an angel giving him a little scroll:

> "Take it, and eat; it will be bitter to your stomach, but sweet as honey in your mouth." So I took the little scroll from the hand of the angel and ate it. (Revelation 10:9-10)

These are wrenching images: tearing apart papyrus with the teeth, enduring the bitter taste of ink. The word of God written, recorded by hand on these ordinary papyrus rolls, becomes something rich and strange and threatening. It is poison to the treacherous and food for the faithful. It is sweet to the taste for the righteous prophet, but bitter medicine for the faithless people who now will hear these words from his mouth. The prophets ingest God's word just as Adam drank God's breath. By its own account, reading the Bible can transform your life, as food transforms your body.

In a gentler, more domesticated form, the prophets' metaphors fed the imagination of English Christians both before and after the Reformation. In his eighth-century *Ecclesiastical History of the English People*, Bede, the great English Benedictine monk and historian, recalls how the illiterate poet Caedmon would memorize Scripture. He would be found "ruminating over it, like some clean animal chewing the cud," and then transform what he heard into "melodious verse." Borrowed from Augustine's *Confessions*, and ultimately traceable to the Torah and the psalms, Bede's striking metaphor is based on a Latin pun. *Ruminare* is what a cow does to its cud, but it is also what a reader does to a book. Bede's playful, domestic pun draws attention to the slowly meditative, "ruminative" methods (called *lectio divina*, or sacred reading) that characterized the study of the Bible as an integral part of the monastic discipline.

Several centuries after Bede, in the blood and smoke of the English Reformation, this ruminative tradition informed the way Archbishop Thomas Cranmer incorporated the daily reading of the Bible into his new English prayer book. Cranmer was firm in his reformer's conviction that the regular reading of Scripture in English was the calling of every English Christian. Bede's metaphor appears again in the homily Cranmer wrote on Scripture for delivery in all parish churches: "Let us ruminate, and, as it were, chew the cud, that we may have the sweet juice, spiritual effect, marrow, honey, kernel, taste, comfort and consolation" of Holy Scripture. The metaphor still lives for contemporary Episcopalians in the Collect on Holy Scriptures that Cranmer first composed for his 1559 prayer book:

> Blessed Lord, who hast caused all holy Scriptures to be written for our learning: Grant that we may in such wise hear them, read, mark, learn, and inwardly digest them; that, by the patience and comfort of your holy Word, we may embrace and ever hold fast the blessed hope of everlasting life. (BCP 184)

Bible reading as chewing the cud; understanding the Bible as an inward digestion. Communion with God is made possible by tasting the sacred page. Reading the Bible offers a contact with God's Word as immediate and intimate as eating.

Consider this story. It is the first Easter day, and two friends of Jesus are walking the seven miles from Jerusalem to Emmaus when they meet a stranger who catches up to them on the road: "What are you discussing with each other while you walk along?" Stung by the stranger's ignorance, they recount in detail how Jesus of Nazareth, a "prophet mighty in deed and word before God and all the people" had been executed by the Roman authorities, and how some women in their group had astounded them with the news that his body was gone; how the same women had seen "a vision of angels" who said that he was alive.

> Then he said to them, "Oh, how foolish you are, and how slow of heart to believe all that the prophets have declared! Was it not necessary that the Messiah should suffer these things and then enter into his glory?" Then beginning with Moses and all the prophets, he interpreted to them the things about himself in all the scriptures. (Luke 24:25-27)

Here, near the conclusion of Luke's gospel, the Christian Bible begins to take shape within our hearing—not as a story written, but as a story told. "Beginning with Moses and all the prophets," the mysterious figure on the road, whom we readers know to be Jesus long before the two pilgrims can recognize him, lays before them the entire trajectory of the scriptures. It is significant that he does so without reference to the written page. In Luke's understanding, voice precedes script: Scripture must be told and heard before it is written and read. And even when told, Scripture has its limits. Hearing Scripture prepares the ground for the encounter with the Holy One, but it does not substitute for it.

As they came near the village to which they were going, he walked ahead as if he were going on. But they urged him strongly, saying, "Stay with us, because it is almost evening and the day is now nearly over." So he went in to stay with them. When he was at the table with them, he took bread, blessed and broke it, and gave it to them. Then their eyes were opened, and they recognized him, and he vanished from their sight. They said to each other, "Were not our hearts burning within us while he was talking to us on the road, while he was opening the scriptures to us?" (Luke 24:28-32)

This central episode in Luke's gospel gives flesh to Jeremiah's metaphor of reading as eating. The holy book that must be learned, marked, read, and inwardly digested is in the end no book at all. It is the very person of the Incarnate One, the Word made flesh, at once the interpreter of the book and its subject. As Jesus said in the synagogue at Nazareth: "Today this scripture has been fulfilled in your hearing" (Luke 4:21). In the end, God's truth is to be found not in the book, but in the presence of the risen Christ, recognized in the breaking of the bread. In other words, we read the book, but in the end it is God who reads us—the living, loving God whose Spirit breathes through Scripture, leaving us with our hearts burning within us.

Opening the Bible provides you with a map and compass as you begin this sacred journey. What you will find in this book is a practical guide to navigating the Bible page. It is meant to be read with an annotated Bible before you (I will say more about that later). Its principal aim is to make the sacred page become more accessible to the ordinary reader. I hope to get those who are beginners past some of the hurdles of their first encounter with matters of format and style so that energies can be given over to reading and rereading what really matters. A related aim, equally important, is to show how the various kinds of notes and scholarly apparatus usually included on the printed page can offer you an entry into a virtual community of readers and religious thinkers—the men and women who have shaped our biblical traditions through several millennia of faithful reading. In particular, this book will introduce Christian readers of the Bible to Jewish traditions of reading in community that would have been familiar to Jesus and Paul. They remain powerful among Jewish readers of the Bible today, and can provide us with a dynamic model for reading it in our own churches.

I offer no shortcuts for answering your deepest questions about what the Bible means. No book can or should. But it can help map the territory. The goal is not to give you ready answers; that would be to subvert this book's purpose, which is to foster conversation and debate, not to cut it off. Rather, the goal is to help you shape the questions. It is meant to nurture your practical competence in reading the Bible, to increase your interest in the Book as a book, to whet your appetite for continued reading, and to deepen your appreciation of the Bible's extraordinary delights. What you have in your hand is literally a handbook, or better, to use that wonderful old Latin word, a *vademecum*—a book that you can take with you as you begin to read the Bible again. Use it as a friendly companion on the Way.

Chapter 2

Preparing to Read

B egin by picking up a Bible. Don't open it yet. Just hold it in your hand and feel its heft, its weight. Think of it as a physical object. Whether produced shabbily or sumptuously, in paperback or bound in leather, modern Bibles are designed to be handled—paged through, manipulated, stroked, prized, purchased, awarded, sold, borrowed, dusted, smelled, venerated, dropped, shelved, marked with yellow highlighter by a college undergraduate, or thumped on a pulpit by an old-time preacher.

Unless your past associations with the Bible make you uneasy, or you are afraid someone will see you with a Bible in your hand and mistake you for a religious fanatic, what you are doing probably seems ordinary, unremarkable. But it isn't ordinary. In fact, the simple act of holding that book in your hand was once considered subversive and revolutionary. In some parts of the world it still is. The Bible is not always what it appears to be.

∼ Scroll and Codex: The Earliest Bibles
What you hold in your hand is a modern invention. As a physical object, your Bible would have puzzled its original writers. In Jesus' day, when most of the materials in the Hebrew Bible had already been written, collected, and

translated into both Aramaic and Greek, no one would have thought of a Bible as we do. Until at least the second century of the Common Era[1] what we call the Bible was not the single bound volume that we know, but several volumes. Isaiah or Jesus or Paul could never have held a single Bible in their hand. They probably would not have used such a word. They would more likely have used a Hebrew or Aramaic or Greek equivalent of the English word "writing," the way we now use the word "scripture" or "scriptures," words derived from the Latin word for writing. And the words they used for reading the Bible would be closer today to a combination of the English words we use to describe "hearing" and "reading aloud."

In Jesus' day, reading from the Hebrew Bible was usually a public event. It would have meant selecting from a score of separate papyrus scrolls kept together in a communal place. (These would have been known in Greek as *ta biblia*, "the little scrolls," whence the English word "Bible.") Once you had access to a scroll, you would have to hold it with two hands, turning one end of the scroll in one hand as you turned the opposite end with the other. This collection of *ta biblia* was the only kind of Bible Jesus and his contemporaries knew. Almost invariably, reading from one of the scrolls would have been a public act, the kind of thing described early in Luke's gospel, when Jesus reads from the Isaiah scroll in his hometown synagogue:

> He stood up to read, and the scroll of the prophet Isaiah was given to him. He unrolled the scroll and found the place where it was written:
>> "The Spirit of the Lord is upon me,
>>> because he has anointed me
>>>> to bring good news to the poor.

> He has sent me to proclaim
>> release to the captives
>> and recovery of sight to the blind,
>> to let the oppressed go free,
>> to proclaim the year of the Lord's favor."
>
> And he rolled up the scroll, gave it back to the attendant, and sat down. The eyes of all in the synagogue were fixed on him. Then he began to say to them, "Today this scripture has been fulfilled in your hearing." (Luke 4:16-21)

What Jesus means here by the word "scripture" is in large measure the theme of this book's final chapter. For now, just notice that the gospel writer does not say explicitly that Jesus read the Isaiah scripture *aloud*. Of course, the episode makes no sense unless he did. Oral reading is simply taken for granted. Long before New Testament times, and well into the Middle Ages, the act of reading aloud is almost invariably implied in the verb "to read." Reading aloud was a common ancient practice, even when reading in solitude or privacy. That ancient custom lies behind our contemporary reading of Scripture, especially in worship.

Within a few generations of Jesus' reading Scripture in synagogue, the technology of the book had begun to change. Christians began to collect stories like Luke's, along with Jesus' sayings and the letters of Paul, in separate anthologies. For reasons that scholars are still debating, they put aside the ancient practice of writing on scrolls and adopted an alternative and relatively rarer method of book-binding, called the *codex*.

A codex (plural, "codices") in some ways closely resembled the Bible you hold in your hand. A scribe would collect the Greek manuscripts of the emerging New Testament

writings (and eventually, the Greek translation of the Hebrew Bible as well), and copy them onto large, folio-sized
leaves made of either papyrus, an early form of paper, or
specially-cured animal skins called *vellum*, or parchment.
These leaves would then be folded and bound together in
large folio volumes. Perhaps the early church turned to the
codex to distinguish its Bible, consisting now of an Old and
New Testament, from the Bibles used by Jews. Perhaps it
was meant to facilitate their work as missionaries, since
much of what the Christians preached in the Gentile world
relied on specific passages from sacred Jewish writings, and
it was useful to have copies in Greek at hand. Even rabbinical Judaism, emerging in Palestine, Syria, Egypt, Babylon
(present-day Iran and Iraq), and elsewhere after the destruction of the Jerusalem temple in 70 CE, eventually
adopted the codex format for its extensive commentaries
on the Hebrew Bible, which came to be known collectively
as the Talmud. But Jews never relinquished the scroll as the
medium for reading the Bible in synagogue worship.

Thus from the start, the codex was the characteristic
format for the new Christian writings. Over the course of
the centuries only a very few of the early Greek codices
have survived intact, although there are scores of manuscript fragments. By the fifth century, the Greek Bible
began to be displaced among western Christians by the
great Latin translation of St. Jerome, known as the Vulgate.
Jerome's Latin Bible became the official Bible of the western
church. Often sumptuously produced, codices of the Vulgate multiplied throughout western Europe, and would
enter the collections of congregations, basilicas, cathedrals,
monasteries, the royal courts, and the emerging universities. But important as they were, these great codices were
all but invisible to ordinary people, most of whom were
illiterate.

Both scrolls and codices were expensive to make, and therefore rare. Reading them was a major enterprise, demanding different kinds of skills and different kinds of expectations from those we bring to the books we so easily take down from our shelves. Until Renaissance and Reformation times, the large, expensive manuscript codex was the only form the Christian Bible took in the west. Although there were many small and exquisite prayer books and Books of Hours created for the private devotions of the very rich in the Middle Ages, as well as great choir scores and liturgical books, the Bible was unique. Everything about it—its size, its cost, its rarity, its Latinity, its difficulty, its very sacredness—made the Bible for most of its history in the western world a book set apart.

∾ The Portable Book

The invention of the printing press did not immediately change all this. Even when Gutenberg produced the first printed Bible, using the newly invented process of movable type, the book was still a massive and forbidding thing. Printed in two magnificent folio volumes in late 1455 or early 1456, Gutenberg's Latin Bible outwardly looked much the same as a codex. Like most of the first printed Bibles, it was designed to resemble the large manuscript volumes that were available only in the great European churches, monasteries, and institutions of learning, or in the private collections of the wealthy. The first printers even designated specific places to be left blank on the page, so that artists could paint them in, making the finished product look more like an illuminated manuscript. Even the typeface was designed to resemble the thick curves and elaborate serifs of Gothic script (known as black-letter type). The book was a gorgeous, precious object, expensive, large, and scarce.

In the 1490s, the great Venetian printer Aldus Manutius invented what he called an *enchiridion*, from the Greek words for "in the hand"—in short, a portable book. The effect of this innovation was breathtaking. These elegant books, printed in the clean cursive typeface known as italic, made readily available for the first time in centuries the great classics of Greek and Roman culture. Before presses like the Aldine were founded, these works could be consulted only in the awkward scrolls of antiquity (very few of which survived) and the large bound codices of the Middle Ages. Free of elaborate commentary, printed in a clear new typeface, books from the Aldine Press remain both beautiful objects in their own right and models of books made for intensive private use. Johannes Gutenberg may have invented the printing press, but it was Aldus Manutius who paved the way for the convenience and accessibility of the book as we know it.

Aldus did not publish a Bible in this attractive new format; perhaps he considered Bibles too holy to handle so casually. The large Bibles he did publish, though, are masterpieces of humanist scholarship and the bookmaking craft, and they played a powerful role in facilitating the new Bible translations—first from the Latin, and then from the Hebrew and Greek—that were about to turn Europe upside down. But the Aldine Bibles themselves were still reserved for the learned and the privileged. The portable format might be suitable for publishing the newly rediscovered and newly edited texts of classical Greece and Rome, but Bibles were a weightier matter. Renaissance humanists like Aldus Manutius gave the portable book its size and shape, but it took the great Protestant reformers to give it its own theology.

Aldus's conservatism was short-lived. Within a decade or two, with Luther and other Protestant reformers insisting that the Bible be made accessible to every believer, the Bible had been translated into German, French, English, and other European languages, and would soon be published in a portable format for mass consumption. This once-privileged book could now become the personal possession of ordinary people, many of whom were becoming literate enough to read it. By the end of the sixteenth century, to publish a Bible or to buy it you no longer needed the privilege of great wealth or the sanction of a great institution like the church or the crown. For better or worse, the Bible was now an openly available commodity in the marketplace of ideas.

It did not become so without controversy and bloodshed. When the Bishop of London, traveling through Antwerp, bought up every copy he could find of William Tyndale's bold new translation of the New Testament, he thought he could put an end to such seditious behavior by sending the copies back to London to be burned publicly in Cheapside. What he didn't know was that Tyndale himself had been made aware of the plan, and secretly cooperated: "for being about [preparing] a more correct edition, he found he would be better enabled to proceed, if the copies of the old were sold off; he therefore gave the merchant all he had, and Tunstall, paying for them, brought them over to England, and burned them."[2] Tyndale's entrepreneurial sleight of hand provides a rare moment of humor in what was for him deadly serious business. It did not take long for people to realize that if you could own your own book, if you could hold it in your hand, if you could read it in your own language, then you could also interpret it in your own way, no matter what the bishop or the pope or even the king might say. Reading a Bible on your own could run you a great risk. It could even bring you to the stake, as it brought Tyndale.

We are still living with the results of that tumultuous period in the history of the printed book. The fact that you can hold a printed Bible in your hand at all, and read it in English, and make your own decisions about how to interpret it results from the extraordinary cunning, courage, and self-sacrifice of sixteenth-century reformers like William Tyndale.

There is something puzzling about all this. For centuries before Tyndale's printed Bible made its first appearance, the Bible had been a rare and sacred object, made by holy hands, passed reverently from generation to generation, read and interpreted only in community. One would have thought that its mechanical reproduction in the age of print would have in some way diminished its power and sacredness. The printed book, marketed as a commodity, distanced by countless middlemen from the circumstances of its first creation, would seem much more impersonal than a codex or a manuscript. It would lack the aura attached to it by the time and care of the monk who prepared it, or the monastery that preserved it, or the cathedral school that maintained the traditions of reading it properly. It would no longer have a permanent place in a monastic or collegiate library among other rare and treasured manuscripts, passed from hand to hand by generations of scholars. It would no longer be interpreted by and for the specific community in which it was lodged. Wouldn't availability breed contempt?

In fact the opposite happened. The printed Bible became an object of immense cultural power. The shift from manuscript to printed book, at least in the early days of the Reformation, intensified rather than diminished its aura: "The printed word had a kind of absoluteness, integrity and finality...an intensity, a shaping power" that was a new experience in western culture.[3] It was a power all the more intense for individual readers who began to interpret the Bible freely and for themselves, and viewed that freedom as their birthright.

Can its power still be felt today? I think it can. But first Episcopalians have to learn how to open the book again, and this is not as easy as it seems. Most of us own a Bible, but few know what to do with it. What keeps people ignorant of the Bible is not an unwillingness to tackle its complexities (in my experience as a teacher, people are willing to tackle all kinds of things), but rather one of two assumptions. Either they think that the Bible is an ancient and forbidding book accessible only to experts—to historians, philologists, theologians, archeologists, linguists, ministers, and priests—or they think that it is accessible only to true believers, offering a refuge for people (ministers and priests included) who mistrust the intellect and seek to keep new ideas at bay.

This book offers some alternative assumptions. Although any responsible reading of an ancient text needs the support of experts in a variety of disciplines, the tools exist for any competent reader to take advantage of the experts' discoveries and insights. There is no need to be intimidated. Furthermore, even though the Bible has a long history of being used as a weapon against people with whom we disagree or whom we fear or hate, it is larger than the use people make of it. So there is no need to be intimidated in this quarter, either.

What do you really need to open the Bible and to read it well? Not a lot, when you come right down to it. You start with a conviction that God speaks to us through the Bible, and a prayerful disposition to listen. And then you bring an open heart, an open mind, a willingness to learn and to make mistakes, a respect for other readers' views, a tolerance for differences of opinion, and a love of surprises.

And you'll need some decent tools. In the following chapters, I will take you on a guided tour of an annotated English-language Bible. Each feature of the printed Bible page has a history and a purpose: the running head, the numbering of chapter and verse, the varied typography, the translators' notes, the layout in columns, the commentary. All these are stops on the tour. We will also follow up several intriguing detours along the way, from the ancient Jewish methods of reading to the production history of a Shakespeare play. The annotated Bible I will cite most often is the *New Oxford Annotated Bible*, also known as the NOAB, the "Oxford Annotated," or simply "the Oxford."[4] The NOAB is one of the most widely used study Bibles in this country. In the way it lays out the page, it is a direct descendant (although much changed) of both the Geneva Bible of 1560 and the English Bible that King James commissioned in 1604. Because it uses the *New Revised Standard Version* (the NRSV) as its copy text, the NOAB can trace its lineage back to William Tyndale's translations and commentaries of the 1520s and 1530s.

Perhaps because of its roots in the Tyndale, Geneva, and King James traditions, the NRSV is the translation most widely used in public worship in the Episcopal Church. My discussion will make more sense if you have the Oxford Annotated open before you, but most other modern annotated Bibles have similar features. Particularly useful ones are the latest editions of the *Harper/Collins Study Bible* (also based on the NRSV), the *New Jerusalem Bible*, the *Oxford Study Bible*, the *Catholic Study Bible*, and the *NIV Study Bible*, based on the *New International Version*. I have consulted all of them in preparing this book, and it can be used profitably with any of them.

Now open your Bible, to any page at random. Don't be daunted by what you see. In the next few chapters, you will find that the page is less formidable than it looks. Learning to use the tools of the annotated page will equip you to engage in spirited conversation with other readers across the centuries, including the biblical writers themselves. In fact, we will see that the best models for reading the Bible as Scripture can be found in the Bible itself, in episodes like King Josiah's discovery of the scroll of the Law during the restoration of the Temple in 2 Kings 23 or the apostle Philip's encounter with the Ethiopian eunuch in Acts 8. By learning to recognize ourselves as participants in scenes of reading like these, we can help nurture larger and more hospitable communities of faith.

Chapter 3

Scanning the Page

O pen your Bible to Jeremiah 15:15, and then to Mark 16:8. Notice I do not provide page numbers. If you compare two or three Bibles, you will notice that the page numbers vary considerably from one edition to another, creating the need for a standard reference system. References are therefore usually given by chapter and verse: chapter numbers are to the left of the colon or period, verse numbers to the right. But page numbers do appear, and can be helpful in finding your way from one book of the Bible to another. Tables of contents usually list the books of the Hebrew Bible and the New Testament separately, both alphabetically and in traditional order, and provide the relevant page numbers. The Oxford tables of contents are included in the material at the beginning of the volume, beginning at page xxiv. The Jeremiah page referred to in these discussions is p. 987 OT (that is, Old Testament); the page for Mark 16 is p. 74 NT (or New Testament). It is not unusual for study Bibles to number the Old Testament and New Testament pages separately, a practice new Bible readers may find confusing at first.

~ The Running Head

Take a moment to look at the page itself, just as a page. When you begin scanning it from the top, the first feature you encounter is what printers and compositors call the "running head," with the title of the book you are reading. When printing a book, the running head allows compositors to keep track of the various pages in the process of collation and binding. A feature of the printed page that most readers take for granted, it points up one of the primary ways the technology of the printed book changed the way the Bible could be read. As we saw in chapter one, in ancient times the "book" of Jeremiah would actually have been written on a separate papyrus or vellum scroll, accessible on a shelf with other similar scrolls containing other sacred texts. When Christians adopted the codex as the form for their Bibles, it became necessary to remind readers which of the various books they were reading.

Most readers of printed books are so accustomed to the convenience of the present system that it is virtually invisible. Editorial conventions like running heads make it easy for contemporary readers to leaf back and forth from book to book, comparing and contrasting passages. Our ancient counterparts did not have this advantage, relying instead on their extraordinary skills in recalling the content of other writings still on the shelf as they worked with the scroll in their hands.

How did the books get their titles?

Although few things in life seem more familiar, titles such as Genesis, Exodus, Mark, and John are by and large a late innovation. Most books of the Bible were originally called something else, or had no titles at all. Moreover, the titles of books in our printed editions can still vary among Anglicans, Protestants, Orthodox, Roman Catholics, and

Jews. For example, Christian Bibles like the Oxford refer to the second book of the Old Testament (itself a Christian term) as the book of Exodus, a title used in the fourth-century BCE Greek translation of the Hebrew Bible called the Septuagint. Hebrew Bibles, on the other hand, kept to the older practice of calling each of the first five books by the first words of its opening sentence—in the case of Exodus, *We'elleh semot*, "And these are the names." Since the Hebrew Bible lived as much in the oral memory of the reader as on the page, remembering the first words allowed the reader to connect the recitation of the book of Exodus with the recitation of the book that had come immediately before—*Bereshith*, "In the beginning," which is the Hebrew title of the book of Genesis.

A similar phenomenon occurs with the fourth book of the Bible. Most English translations of the Hebrew Bible, Christian or Jewish, follow the Septuagint in giving it the title *Arithmoi*, or Numbers, since so much of the early part of the book is devoted to reports of various censuses. But in the Hebrew Bible the title is once again taken from the first word of the book, *Bemidbar*, "In the wilderness." Similarly, the book of Leviticus, whose name in the Greek Bible designates the Levitical code that makes up much of the book's subject matter, is in Hebrew *Wayyiqra'*, "And he summoned." Deuteronomy, which is Greek for "the second Law," is called in Hebrew *Debarim*, "These are the words." Most English translations of the Hebrew Bible, whether Christian or Jewish, now follow the Greek model for naming these books, perhaps because the first English Bibles did so in the sixteenth century.

In the New Testament, the gospels came by their names quite late; the texts first appeared anonymously. The names of the four evangelists were assigned by later traditions, and have little or no historical basis. Luke's gospel is unusual in that it is the only one to appear in two separate volumes, the second called the Acts of the Apostles. In the traditional order of the New Testament books, Acts is separated from Luke by the gospel of John. Although we do not know who wrote the gospels according to Matthew, Mark, Luke, and John, we now think we know something about the different communities for which they were written and which great ancient metropolitan centers might have been associated with them—Mark with Alexandria, for example, and Matthew with Antioch in present-day Turkey. I will refer to the gospel writers using the traditional names, but it is important to bear in mind that these names have more to do with traditions of reading than with the gospels' actual authorship.

The case with Paul's writings is almost the opposite. From the beginning Paul's name was attached to the several letters attributed to him, but recent scholars generally agree that not all the letters bearing his name are actually his. Most think that there are seven authentic letters of Paul: 1 Thessalonians, Galatians, 1 Corinthians, 2 Corinthians, Romans, Philippians, and Philemon. The authorship of Colossians and Ephesians is more uncertain, but most scholars are convinced that 1 Timothy, 2 Timothy, and 2 Thessalonians are products of a Pauline "school"—a group of Paul's followers most likely writing in the generation following his death.

Writing a letter using a famous name seems odd and dishonest to us, who are so used to grappling with issues of copyright, plagiarism, and intellectual property. But the practice was quite common in the ancient world, and was considered a way of honoring the memory of a movement's founder. Most scholars think that letters attributed to Peter, Jude, James, and John follow the same pattern. No name is given to the writer of the letter to the Hebrews, however.

A remarkable document, written by a person deeply versed in Jewish liturgical practice, this letter stands by itself in the collection. And although the Revelation to John is often ascribed to the writer of John's gospel, and to John the disciple who plays such a central role in it, most scholars doubt this attribution on grounds of style.

How did the books get their final shape?

The content and shape of the biblical books as we now know them, particularly the books of the Hebrew Bible, took centuries to develop and are often the product of a long series of editorial decisions made by various communities of teachers and readers over several generations. Scholars tell us that the "book" of Jeremiah is in fact a compendium of several different kinds of writing, not all of which are actually "by" the author Jeremiah in the way that we are accustomed to understand authorship. As happened later in the New Testament period, the name of a great prophet like Jeremiah or Isaiah could be attached not only to their own sayings and writings, but also to writings composed generations later. Sometimes these writings were produced by the prophet's direct followers, who reinterpreted and reapplied the prophetic words to their own times; sometimes they are the product of a believing community that, inspired by the earlier writings, sought to put its own religious practices under the patronage of the prophet it revered.

Finally, the very order of the books varies with the different traditions. By the second century before the Common Era, the writings of the Hebrew Bible had more or less coalesced into three separate collections. There was the *Torah*, ("The Teaching" or "The Law" or "The Way"), consisting of the first five books of the Bible. Tradition attributed their authorship to Moses himself, even though the fifth book, Deuteronomy, describes his death. Anomalies like this are what first prompted eighteenth- and nineteenth-century scholars to unravel and describe the various literary traditions, sometimes widely separated in time and purpose, that eventually were woven together in the Torah that has come down to us. As we will see in a later chapter, this "higher criticism" of the Bible has had a tremendous impact on the way people learn to read Scripture.

The second collection of sacred writings, in Hebrew called *Nebi'im* ("The Prophets"), includes not only the writings of the prophets contained in books like Jeremiah and Isaiah, but also what we would call the historical books like 1 and 2 Kings. And finally there are the *Ketubim* ("The Writings), including the Psalms and Wisdom literature, some of which were composed under the influence of Persian and Greek religious thinking as recently as a few centuries before the birth of Christ. Jewish readers often refer to Torah, Nebi'im, and Ketubim together, using the acronym *Tanakh*, compounded from the initial consonant in each word.

The Christians, however, reshaped the order of Jewish scriptures in response to what they saw as the fulfillment of prophecy in the events surrounding Christ's death and resurrection. The Christian Bible begins as the Hebrew Bible does, with the book of Genesis, but shuffles the order of books in such a way that the last book of what Christians call the Old Testament, the book of Malachi, can be read as a kind of apocalyptic prelude to the gospel of Matthew, which in most Christian Bibles immediately follows.

In some Bibles you will notice a section of writings placed between the Old Testament and the New Testament, or sometimes at the end of the entire volume. These writings are referred to as the *Apocrypha* (from the Greek— "things hidden"). The Apocrypha includes writings that appeared in the Greek and Latin versions but were never part of the traditional Hebrew text that formed the basis of the first Protestant translations. The Episcopal Church still uses some of these writings in its Sunday worship and daily office, without granting them the same inspired status as the officially recognized or "canonical" writings.

What was left out?

Printed Bibles, even those as voluminous as the Oxford Annotated, seldom give the reader a hint that both Jews and Christians once considered other writings equal in stature to the books that were eventually included in their Bibles. In recent years, there has been a tremendous amount of attention paid to the library of ancient Christian and gnostic documents discovered in 1945 in the Egyptian desert, near a little settlement called Nag Hammadi. "Gnostic" is derived from the set of Greek words denoting knowledge, here particularly secret knowledge; a gnostic is "one who knows." Although written mainly in the ancient Ethiopian language called Coptic, and able to be dated to two or three centuries after New Testament times, some of these documents are actually translations of early Greek material that may reflect other directions the Christian movement was taking in its earliest years. At least one of these documents, known as the gospel of Thomas, includes material that presents parallels to materials found in what are called the four canonical gospels (from the Greek *kanon*, "rule" or "standard").

These are very exciting materials to read, and very puzzling. Work on the Nag Hammadi documents has reshaped many people's thinking about the nature of the Bible itself. When scanning the running heads and considering the variety of biblical books, it is well to remember that what got into the Bible and what did not was often the result of highly contested institutional decisions. The Christian Bible in its final form has rightly been called "the church's book." In the light of the tremendous intellectual, political, cultural, and religious ferment that these new documents reflect, we might also say that the Bible you hold in your hands is the book put together by the winners.

I usually employ the phrase "Hebrew Bible" or "Hebrew scriptures" to refer to the body of writings in Hebrew and Aramaic that comprise the *Tanakh*, the Bible used by Jews throughout the world. I do this not only because the Hebrew Bible has its own literary and theological integrity, but also because it is a more convenient way to refer to the body of writing that Jesus, Paul, and their immediate followers would themselves have called Scripture.

Thematic headings

One final note before we leave the top of the page. Many printed Bibles in English also provide some sort of thematic heading at the top of the page to guide the reader through complex material. Like chapter and verse numbering, these headings are not original to the texts. In modern Bibles like the Oxford Annotated, the headnotes provide a terse synopsis of the content to be found on the page: *Jeremiah complains again and is reassured; the empty tomb*. Historically, printed Bibles have also used these headnotes, along with chapter and section headings, to help the reader navigate the page not only textually but theologically. In study Bibles like the Oxford, they are offered, like the running head, only to facilitate efficient navigation of the page. Use them accordingly.

❧ Citing Chapter and Verse

Almost from the first, printed Bibles adopted a system of numbering chapters that had been used in manuscript

Bibles since the time of Stephen Langton, Archbishop of Canterbury in the fourteenth century. We are so used to thinking of the various books of the Bible as divided into chapters that it is difficult to imagine having them any other way, but chapter divisions are relatively late in the history of the Bible, and were not part of the original Hebrew, Aramaic, and Greek texts. As we will see, the earliest Greek manuscripts do not even separate words on the page, much less include any larger divisions.

The numbering of separate verses came even later than the division into chapters. A Rabbi Nathan began the practice in the Middle Ages, and it was further extended by the humanist scholar Robert Estienne in 1551. Verse numbers first appeared in a printed English Bible six years later, in the New Testament published by English Protestant exiles in Geneva during the reign of the Roman Catholic Queen Mary. Chapter and verse divisions have been with us ever since.

They have proved a mixed blessing. Without question, they are indispensable for negotiating complex and voluminous biblical material. But they can also obscure the meaning of a text rather than clarify it. Sometimes chapter divisions break up narratives that should be read continuously (see, for example, the arbitrary placement of the chapter ending in 2 Samuel 11). Sometimes they give the impression of a continuous narrative when there is none; this happens quite frequently in the gospels, when Jesus' sayings are quoted at length with only tenuous connection to the story being told (see, for example, Matthew 25). The lectionary of the Episcopal Church (like the Roman Catholic and the Lutheran) often ignores chapter divisions in the readings selected for a given day from the Old and New Testaments. One should not make too much of chapter divisions in trying to interpret a particular text. They are editorial additions, nothing more.

Midrash and allegory

In the ancient world, there was no such thing as giving the precise location of a particular passage by reference to chapter and verse numbers. Nonetheless, both Jewish and Christian commentators on the Bible in the first centuries of the Common Era developed highly sophisticated methods of strategic quotation and commentary. Even within the Hebrew Bible itself, writers of later books like Chronicles in effect reimagined and revised the earlier historical texts found in the books of Samuel and Kings. In intertestamental times (between 250 BCE and 200 CE), multiple methods of reading the Bible flourished. By the time of Jesus and Paul, the Hebrew of the Bible had been translated into the more widely spoken languages of Greek and Aramaic. The Aramaic translation known as the *Targum* was more a paraphrase than a translation, incorporating its own theological point of view into its version of the text. When Jesus read in the synagogue, it is possible that he used the Targum as the starting place for his dramatic reinterpretation of Scripture.

The Greek translation attracted readers versed in Platonic methods of allegorical reading, where the literal sense of the sacred text was merely a mask for its real, hidden meaning, to be uncovered by the reader with special training and insight. These methods were particularly widespread in Greek-speaking Jewish communities like that in Alexandria, where the philosopher Philo produced powerfully influential allegorical readings of Genesis and other Old Testament texts. Philo wrote at about the same time that Paul was composing his letters, which often feature similar allegorical strategies. Paul actually uses the word "allegory" in Galatians 4, where he discusses the stories in Genesis about Sarah and Hagar, whom he sees as representing the old covenant (Hagar) and the new (Sarah).

Even more radical readings of Scripture were produced by apocalyptic Jewish sects like those gathered at Qumran, where the Dead Sea scrolls were produced. Using a method known as *pesher*, the Qumran writers quoted key texts in Scripture and then interpreted them as a kind of code for events happening in their own day, or events about to happen. New Testament scholars recognize this strategy in the way the gospel writers weave earlier biblical texts into their own narratives. Although the differences are great, the method is analogous to what we experience in our own day in the predictions of geopolitical disasters that writers like Hal Lindsay claim to discover in the book of Revelation.

After the destruction of the Temple in Jerusalem by the Romans during the first Jewish revolt in 70 CE, the Pharisees and their successors in the later rabbinical movement embraced an immensely sophisticated method of reading called *midrash*. It is a word hard to translate, but is closely related to English words like "research" and "searching." Since the texts of the Bible were now complete, and all portions of it were considered equally holy, midrashists could focus on the biblical verse as a basic unit. Once the protocols of midrashic reading were agreed upon (and they could be elaborate), it was safe to assume that any verse of the Bible could illuminate any other verse, no matter what the context.

This assumption unleashed remarkable religious energies, as the act of reading Scripture became an exercise in dialogue. The more rabbis there were applying midrashic methods to a biblical verse, the more room there was for disagreement about what other verses could be used to interpret it. But as all verses of Scripture were equally holy and (at least in potential) equally pertinent, there was no need to decide among the rival readings. More often than not, all rival interpretations were incorporated into the midrashic record, and the meaning of the Bible verse at hand would be found in the interplay among them. The act of reading Scripture was less an effort to defend a single, unitary meaning than it was a participation in a lively community of readers, continuing across generations.

A central conviction of the midrashic sensibility is that God's voice, hidden in the sacred text, can be heard in the midst of the human voices reading the texts. As long as all readers agreed to the protocols of midrashic reading, no one voice had absolute or automatic priority over another. Many of these voices are recorded in the rich collections of writings known traditionally as the "oral law" (supplementing and interpreting the "written law" of the Torah), and collected over several centuries in the Talmud and other writings. They can also be heard in the extraordinary collection of medieval Jewish mystical writings known collectively as the *Kabbalah*. The continuing study of the oral law over the centuries has nourished a tradition of sacred reading in contemporary Judaism that allows the reader of Scripture to enter into dialogue with these ancient voices as they come to terms with the sacred text. Especially in Conservative and Reform Judaism, this has meant that conversation about the meaning of Torah is always open and expanding. The function of this Oral Law is "to soften the rigidity of the letter without...violating its sacredness (whence not a jot or a tittle will be allowed to pass away)."[1] The midrashist's open-ended commitment to the necessity of dialogue provides a compelling model for contemporary readers of the Bible, Jewish and Christian alike.

Although Paul's New Testament letters predate these portions of the Talmud by several generations, we can still discern a strong midrashic sensibility at work in the way he quotes and interprets the Bible. Paul's letters are full of quotations from the Septuagint. As they are seldom verbatim, we can assume that for the most part he quotes from memory. It is difficult for late twentieth-century readers to imagine knowing so much of the Bible "by heart," but our dependence upon the written and printed word as an aid to memory was foreign to ancient sensibilities. The sound and rhythm of the sacred writings were part of the warp and woof of memory for anyone trained as a Pharisee, as Paul himself was trained. Paul's love for the sound of Scripture is audible on every page.

But in key passages of his letters, Paul's midrashic love for the sound and letter of the holy words gives way to an allegorical impulse that seeks the spirit "beneath" or "behind" the text. "Our competence is from God," he wrote to his congregation in Corinth, "who has made us competent to be ministers of a new covenant, not of letter but of spirit; for the letter kills, but the Spirit gives life" (2 Corinthians 3:5-6).

Now if the ministry of death, chiseled in letters on stone tablets, came in glory so that the people of Israel could not gaze at Moses' face because of the glory of his face, a glory now set aside, how much more will the ministry of the Spirit come in glory?... Since, then, we have such a hope, we act with great boldness, not like Moses, who put a veil over his face to keep the people of Israel from gazing at the end of the glory that was being set aside. But their minds were hardened. Indeed, to this very day, when they hear the reading of the old covenant, that same veil is still there, since only in Christ is it set aside. Indeed, to this very day whenever Moses is read, a veil lies over their minds; but when one turns to the Lord, the veil is removed. (2 Corinthians 3:7-8, 12-16)

This is both a luminous reading and an outrageous misreading of Exodus 24, where Moses descends with the stone tablets of the Law from Mount Sinai and wearing a veil over his face to protect the people of Israel from being blinded by the glory of God. Here Paul is working in allegory. Instead of quoting the Exodus passage verbatim and then working through it point by point to expand its meaning from within, he neglects the specifics of language and context in order to reveal the real meaning he sees below the surface of the story. For Paul, convinced that the old covenant has given way to the new, what Moses hides with the veil is not a glory too radiant to bear, but a glory that is fading.

In subordinating the "letter" of the Torah, "chiseled in letters on stone tablets" to the new Torah, written on "tablets of human hearts" (2 Corinthians 3:3), Paul uses what look like midrashic methods of quotation to undermine the main purpose of midrash, which is to see in the very letter of Scripture a universe of meaning. Rather than seeing *into* the text, Paul wants his congregation to see *through* it, as all who read the scriptures "in Christ" can see through the veil that Moses put on his face to hide his fading glory—that is, the fading glory of the text that Moses wrote.[2]

This tension between midrash and allegory, between seeing into and seeing through, is a prominent feature in the history of reading the Bible. It is still with us today. For Christian readers after Paul, Hebrew scriptures became the Old Testament. The sacred account of God's saving actions in Israel could be fully understood—in fact, completed—only by their fulfillment in the New Testament writings about Jesus. By the end of the second century, this new approach to the Hebrew Bible had caused an all but irreparable rift between Jew and Christian in their reading of the sacred texts they shared. In many ways, the tension between these two ways of reading still separates not only Christians from Jews, but many Christians from each other.

~ Some Typographical Conventions

Why print the page in columns?

Go back now to the printed Bible page. What does it feel like? That seems an odd question. But books, after all, are tactile objects, and readers of books often have strong tactile memories of them. All books have a heft and feel of their own. Massive books with thin pages printed in columns have the heft and feel of Bibles even if they are not, like complete editions of Shakespeare plays. Pages in Bibles without columns, like the first unannotated edition of the New Testament in the *New English Bible*, look more like the pages of contemporary novels than what we are accustomed to think of as Bibles.[3]

How a page looks and feels determines how we read it. Different printed formats encourage different kinds of reading. Contemporary readers expect that Bibles will be produced on thin leaves of paper and the pages printed in columns, but that is not necessarily the case. Reading a Bible page that looks like a page of a novel will focus our attention on the plot; we will "read for the story." This can be a tremendous revelation to people for whom the Bible has always been a forbidding code of rules. To see the story of Jesus looking like a real story with a beginning, a middle, and an end, to read it without verse numbers or headings or notes, without having to squint at closely packed columns—all this can free people to read the Bible as if for the first time.

But sometimes this ease of reading can be deceptive. Reading a novel for the story encourages you to move quickly from one page to another, to see what happens next, even though most novels of any complexity at all often force you to backtrack, to reconsider, to recognize a symbol or a leitmotif and reassess what you have read so far. Yet the Bible is not written like novel, even a complex one. The novel is a modern form, impossible to imagine without the advent of printing and publishing for profit, while the Bible is an ancient book, large portions of which began as oral tradition, lodged in memory and retold from generation to generation. It was written not by one hand, but by many; not in one lifetime, but over many. It was written in ancient languages—Hebrew, Aramaic, and Greek—many of whose nuances have long been lost to us. It is not a single story, nor even a collection of stories. It is a collection of all kinds of ancient materials—law codes, songs, proverbs, sagas, genealogies, histories, oracles, lyric poems, letters, prophecies, allegories, apocalypses—all of which demand their own distinctive methods of reading.

The Bible includes some remarkable stories, some of which stand on their own (like the stories of Jonah and Ruth), and some of which, although polished and complete in their own right (like the story of Joseph and his brothers that now ends the book of Genesis), also contribute to a larger story whose coherence and meaning only become clear after we can see the whole. And even that reflection is shaped by the presuppositions of the community for whom the story matters. For the religious reader, the stories in the Bible are true in the way that a story in a novel can never be true. For some readers, this conviction makes any comparison of the Bible to any other kind of writing all but blasphemous. Even for those religious readers (among whom many Episcopalians count themselves) who recognize that many of the stories are "history-like" rather than historical, the "truth" of these stories asserts itself in a manner very different from a novel like Tolstoy's *War and Peace*.

At this point we seem to have come a long way from the simple question of page layout. But as often in the religious life, small matters reveal large ones. The traditional format of the Bible, columns and all, is a small but eloquent measure of the tremendous challenge that all the different forms of Scripture have always posed to ordinary readers. Most of us need these tools. All the Bible's apparatus invites you to slow your reading down, and allows you to treat the page spatially, comparing and contrasting complementary texts, meditating on the way that biblical texts echo and refer to one another. You can more easily maneuver across the large amount of material laid out before you on a double page, marked with all kinds of apparatus to guide the reading as it proceeds. Perhaps you've had a similar experience in reading an annotated novel in a student edition, or in reading the text of a Shakespeare play in a "complete" edition, which is often printed in columns and accompanied by voluminous notes, thus giving it the same classic air of authority as a printed Bible. It is no accident that scholarly editions of classic English authors have adapted the kind of page format and annotations that had once been features exclusive to Bibles and other sacred writings like the Talmud.

Even more important, the annotations on the printed page allow you to enter into conversation with the community of readers (some believers, some not) who have preserved and shaped these texts, and to do so in a way that frees you to add your own voice to the chorus. To be sure, the decision to print a long text like the Bible in column formatting was in part a matter of convenience and cost-cutting. It allowed printers to include an immense amount of material in manageable form, especially if the book was to be held easily in the hand. Yet this double column format is also a potent reminder of the close connection of printed Bibles to their earlier manuscript versions. The great medieval codices of Scripture, as well as the parchment scrolls that preceded them, were almost always produced in columns, oftentimes sumptuously illuminated by hand. These were volumes meant for slow reading, usually reading aloud in community. They were in fact community property, rare and precious, and like the great Jewish commentaries to which they are related, their pages reflect century after century of sustained meditation on the sacred text. When you open to a Bible page printed in columns and arrayed with commentary, you are being invited to take part in an ancient enterprise of community reading.

The use of italics

Bible publishers have always used different typefaces to convey features of the Hebrew or Greek text that might otherwise be obscured in translation. We have already become acquainted with the typefaces used by Gutenberg and Aldus in the first printed books. Both Gutenberg's black-letter type and Aldus's italics were meant to imitate the effect of a handwritten page. But a whole page of italic typeface, even one as clean and elegant as Aldus designed, tends to weary the eye. Eventually italic began to be used only sparingly, usually to emphasize particular words or set off annotations and commentary.

Even so, the occurrence of italic type was once much more frequent than it is in today's Bibles. Readers of some editions of the King James translation of 1611 are sometimes confused by what seems to be the random use of italics. For instance, look at Jeremiah 15:18: "Why is my pain perpetual, and my wound incurable, *which* refuseth to be healed? wilt thou be altogether unto me as a liar, *and as* waters *that* fail?" Anyone attempting to read the italicized words with emphasis will come up with nonsense. The italics have another purpose here. Adopting a convention first used by the English Protestant exiles who created the Geneva Bible a generation before, the English translators commissioned by King James in the early 1600s used italics to warn the reader that these words had no equivalent in the Hebrew or Greek text. The translators added them in order to make the English read more smoothly and idiomatically.

The practice was confusing, and later translators eventually dropped it, finding other ways to signal gaps between the original text and its translated equivalents. But its use illustrates the precautions one must take in reading any Bible translation. The way the Geneva and King James translators used italic type reflected the ancient conviction that each word of the original Hebrew or Greek text was of itself sacred and inviolable. Therefore the translator's addition to the text must be marked as such, lest anyone accord to these extra words the same prestige as the sacred words themselves deserve. It was a practice both pious and conservative, but it also signaled something new: these meticulous marks of the translator's interventions underscored the newfound respect that the English Protestant reformers had for the integrity of ancient texts, a respect they inherited from the great Renaissance humanists of the fifteenth century. Their decision to use italic type in this way was in fact a thoroughly modern breakthrough, opening the way for capable and curious readers to return to the original texts themselves as they sought to understand God's word.

In other words, the text is sacred, but no translation is. No translator is fully adequate to the task. All readers in one way or another participate in the practice of translation. Even those who are ignorant of Hebrew and Greek (that is, the vast majority) can compare one translation to another, thereby getting a "feel" for the challenges posed by the original. All translations, however "literal," only approximate the meaning of the Hebrew and Greek texts that they try to render. The King James translators knew this. Their respect for the letter of the original text—and their modesty about their ability to find its exact equivalent in English—continues to be reflected in the translations succeeding theirs, including the *New Revised Standard* text of 1989 that we are using here.

The name of the LORD

A second typographical convention adopted by the early English translators, and found in almost every modern English translation since, including the NRSV, also puzzles many first-time readers of the Bible. It is the use of uppercase letters for the word "Lord," as in this passage from Jeremiah 15:15: "O LORD, you know; remember me and visit me, and bring down retribution for me on my persecutors." In the Hebrew Scriptures God is called by many names: *El, El Shaddai, Adonai, Elohim, Yahweh*. Of all the names for God, it is this last one—*Yahweh*, or more precisely, the Hebrew equivalent of the letters YHWH—that is the most sacred in the tradition. Every time the word YHWH appears in the original Hebrew, the NRSV translators, using a centuries-old typographical convention, signal the occurrence with the word LORD, using all uppercase letters. (A variant of this practice occurs when the Hebrew text uses the phrase "Lord YHWH," which the NRSV renders "Lord GOD.")

It is a typographical procedure fraught with theological implications. In the story of the Exodus, it is the name YHWH that the voice from the burning bush reveals to Moses:

> But Moses said to God, "If I come to the Israelites and say to them, 'The God of your ancestors has sent me to you,' and they ask me, 'What is his name?' what shall I say to them?" God said to Moses, "I AM WHO I AM." He said further, "Thus you shall say to the Israelites, 'I AM has sent me to you.'" God also said to Moses, "Thus you shall say to the Israelites, 'The LORD, the God of your ancestors, the God of Abraham, the God of Isaac, and the God of Jacob, has sent me to you.'" (Exodus 3:13-15)

Ehyeh asher ehyeh: no Bible translator has ever been satisfied with an English rendering of this mysterious Hebrew phrase. The NRSV translators provide two alternatives to the one they adopted: "I AM WHAT I AM," or "I WILL BE WHAT I WILL BE"; they then note that the passage here connects the name YHWH with God's self-revelation, associating it with the Hebrew verb *ehyeh,* "to be."

In the traditional Jewish attitude toward the Bible page, all words are sacred. But none is more sacred than the name YHWH. It is a name not even to be pronounced. When it appears in the portion of the Torah to be read aloud during synagogue worship, the cantor or lector substitutes the word *Adonai* (usually translated as "the Lord" in lower-case letters). In manuscript and printed copies of the Torah, the vowel markings for *Adonai* accompany the consonants YHWH, to remind the reader that *Adonai* is to be read in place of the divine name. (A late medieval misunderstanding of this convention created the unbiblical coinage *Jeho-vah* by combining the consonants of the divine name with the vowels of *Adonai*, and then transliterating accordingly.) Ancient Greek translations of the Hebrew had substituted the word *Kyrios*, "Lord"; the Latin version had used the word *Dominus*. By setting off the word for YHWH in uppercase letters, the English translators pay tribute to this ancient tradition, and continue it. Of all the contemporary English translations, only the Jerusalem Bible broke with the custom, using the word *Yahweh* instead of "The LORD." It was a decision that remains controversial. In the *Book of Common Prayer*, the word *Yahweh* also occurs on occasion, most notably in the Song of Moses (Canticle 8), appointed to be read during the Easter Vigil and suggested as well for daily Morning Prayer. Most observant Jews would find this usage deeply shocking.

J, E, P and D

The conventions I have just described also shed light on the development of the Hebrew texts themselves. All texts have a history, and the more ancient a text, the more complex that history becomes. In the late nineteenth century, a brilliant German scholar named Julius Wellhausen argued in a groundbreaking book that the names used for God in the Hebrew Bible, particularly the names *Yahweh* and *Elo-him*, provide clues to distinctive and separate strands of historical tradition embedded in the documents themselves. For example, those parts of Genesis where the name *Yahweh* is used have a particular stylistic and theological coherence that is distinct from the texts that use the name *Elohim*. The latter in fact is a plural in Hebrew, meaning something like "the gods," although the E tradition (as it is called) gives the word a singular meaning, usually translated simply as "God." Stories using the name *Yahweh* (called the J tradition, from the German spelling *Jahweh*), were probably assembled and edited in the form we now have by a poet writing in the court of David and Solomon (about the year 1000 BCE). A good example of this poet's style of writing is the story of Adam and Eve in the second and third chapters of Genesis. The Elohistic, or E, tradition, on the other hand, is attributed to the religious communities of the Northern Kingdom, which split off from the Jerusalem court after the death of Solomon. Sometimes it is hard to untangle these two separate traditions in the texts as they have come down to us, as they combined and intermingled over the centuries.

In addition, scholars have postulated two other strands of tradition in the development of the texts as we know them—the Priestly (P) and the Deuteronomic (D). The first is associated with the period of the exile in Babylon after the fall of Jerusalem in the sixth century BCE; not surprisingly, these writings are often preoccupied with ritual and cultic matters, including much of the material in the books of Leviticus and Numbers. Perhaps the most moving and eloquent example of the Priestly style is the creation story of the first chapter of Genesis, a highly stylized and radically monotheistic reimagining of the ancient Babylonian creation myths that would have been known to the Priestly writers during the Exile. Lastly, the Deuteronomic tradition is exemplified in the book of Deuteronomy itself, as well as in the history of the Northern and Southern Kingdoms of Israel and Judah as recounted in the books of Samuel and Kings. The Deuteronomic point of view, which is uniformly critical of kingship, has been traditionally associated with the prophetic and reform movements originating in the North but articulated in the circles gathered in Jerusalem in the time of Josiah and later of Jeremiah.

The recognition of these four strands of biblical tradition—J, E, D, and P—for many decades influenced the way
in which the Bible was studied as an historical document.
The hypothesis of multiple traditions has been extraordi-
narily powerful and fruitful, but it has also had its costs.
There has never been full agreement about what texts are
part of what tradition. Many readers worry about the
fragmentation of the biblical text that results from too
assiduous an attempt to isolate the various traditions. More
conservative communities of readers, for whom presuppositions about the unity and inerrancy of Scripture are
theologically paramount, have never been comfortable accepting the insights of the historical criticism that Wellhausen's hypothesis engendered. In recent years, biblical
scholars trained as literary critics have sought different
ways to describe the imaginative and theological coherence
of the biblical text as the Bible has come down to us in its
final form. In describing this biblical "poetics," such readers
have been careful not to return to a precritical point of view
that would deny the tremendous insights that stem from
Wellhausen's momentous discoveries. This reassertion of a
coherent biblical poetics is at the center of current debates
about how to read the Bible.

Chapter 4

Comparing Translations

Among the pitfalls of reading the Bible in English is forgetting that you are reading a translation. *Caveat lector!* Reader, beware! The Bible is the product of a staggering number of linguistic and cultural traditions, dating through many centuries. There is an old saying that the past is a foreign country. That may be so, but its borders are open: the past is accessible to those willing to make the effort to understand it. Likewise, an informed respect for the variety of ancient languages and cultural presuppositions in the Bible is indispensable for understanding the meaning of the texts. In these as in most matters, the more you know the better off you are. It is helpful to be aware of how languages can differ from each other not only in their structure and grammar, but also in their use of words, in their history, and in their characteristic sounds. Different languages have different ways of saying things, and these ways are seldom equivalent or interchangeable.

∼ What Translations Reveal
Annotated Bibles are a window onto some of the challenges every translator faces. Although translators' notes cannot

comment on every interesting word or group of words, they can alert us to the fact that a word or phrase or sentence in the Hebrew or Greek is particularly obscure, or when other manuscript traditions display alternative readings. Translators' notes usually appear at the base of a column of text, above the line separating text from commentary (if there is commentary). They are marked with small-case italic letters in superscript that correlate the note with the verse in question, and this pattern holds in even the most lightly annotated Bibles.

No two translations are alike. All translations are the result of choices made and choices rejected. Gifted translators often disagree. When they do, their disagreements usually center on finding the most faithful English equivalents of complex words or sets of words. Take as an example the Hebrew word *dabar* and the Greek word *logos*. Both can roughly be translated into English as "word" or "speech," but such a translation dangerously simplifies some very complicated nuances. *Dabar* also has meanings closer to "event" or "deed." In Jeremiah 5:28 the prophet says his enemies "know no limits in deeds of wickedness"; the word translated as "deeds" is a form of *dabar*. Compare the English phrase "I give you my word," where saying the word "word" is itself a form of action. It is like saying "I will" at a wedding—saying so makes it so.

The synonym for *dabar* in Greek, *logos*, has different connotations. Like *dabar*, *logos* means "word," but also "reasoning" or "rationality" or something like "the informing principle." The two words are not always equivalent to each other; their meanings can vary according to context. According to one count, the *King James Version* translates *dabar* by seventy-five different words, *logos* by twenty-five. If the words for "word" are this varied and nuanced in the original Hebrew and Greek, imagine how difficult it is to find their exact equivalents in English each time they occur.

Annotated Bibles like the Oxford do not usually tell us when these kinds of decisions are being made. There are too many of them. That is why comparing two or more English translations of the same passage can sometimes be very revealing, and you should have access to at least two different translations when working with a particular text. Even then, there are challenges. Some translations, like the original *Revised Standard*, strive for a more or less literal correspondence between the original language and the English translation. (The technical phrase for this is "formal equivalence.") The NRSV translators use the motto "as literal as possible, as free as necessary," and in fact tend to be freer than their predecessors.[1] Striving for formal equivalence can sometimes make for awkward English sentences, but it helps the reader approximate the "feel" of the Hebrew and Greek. Other translations strive for a more dynamic equivalence, sometimes resorting to paraphrase in a contemporary English idiom. Paraphrase can make for a more readable and accessible text, but sometimes the end result is far removed from the sense and feel of the original. This is often the case with the simplified, informal style of the *Good News Bible*, first published in 1966. Other paraphrases hide theological agendas. *The Living Bible* translates Paul's technical term "righteousness" *(dikaiosūne,* a complex term in Paul) in the language of the tent revival, "getting right with God," while the word for "born" in 1 John 3:9 becomes the more pulpit-friendly "born again."

What translation one prefers is partly a result of taste, and partly of theological conviction. More conservative Protestants have always been wary of modern versions of the King James Bible, such as the *Revised Standard*, perhaps because the liberal National Council of Churches sponsored these revisions. Believing that it strayed too far from what William Tyndale had called the "plain sense" of Scripture, a group of conservative Protestant translators produced the *New International Version* in 1978. The NIV is the first Bible widely regarded in conservative circles as an acceptable successor to the King James, even though the methods of translation do not seem to differ in any substantial way from methods used by the NRSV. It is a mark of this translation's popularity and effectiveness that the General Convention of the Episcopal Church recently added it to the short list of Bible translations officially acceptable for use in public worship. In addition to the *Revised Standard Version* and *New Revised Standard Version* used most widely, the list currently includes the *King James Version*, the *Jerusalem Bible*, the *New English Bible*, the *Good News Bible*, and the *New American Bible*.

~ The Translating Process

Comparing different translations of the same Bible passage often yields some startling surprises. Sometimes the translators even seem to be working from different Bibles. Why is this?

Until the discovery of the Dead Sea Scrolls in the late 1940s, the earliest complete manuscript copies of Hebrew and Christian scriptures dated from the early Middle Ages. While there are many very early papyrus fragments of New Testament books, complete extant manuscripts are relatively late. Furthermore, all modern translations are based on original texts that are themselves the product of generations of readers and scholars sifting, collating, and comparing scores of texts. Even in the standard scholarly editions of both the Hebrew Bible and the Greek New Testament you will find alternative readings on every page, including alternative reconstructions of texts that for various reasons have come down to us in damaged or, as the scholars say, "corrupted" form. Sometimes the editors of the English translations indicate by a special footnote that some textual problem has arisen; we will encounter two intriguing examples of this later in the chapter.

But sometimes the decisions made by editors and translators are invisible. An instructive example of this occurred in the first edition of the *New English Bible* (the NEB), a British translation first published in 1970 with broad ecumenical backing. Look again at the passage from Jeremiah 15. Here is how it reads in the NRSV:

> Your words were found, and I ate them,
>   and your words became to me a joy
>   and the delight of my heart;
> for I am called by your name,
>   O LORD, God of hosts. (Jeremiah 15:16)

The wording reproduced here can be found in almost all English translations and is based on the Hebrew text as it appears in the most widely used scholarly edition. But if you look up the verse in the 1970 NEB, you will encounter a very different image:

> I have to suffer those who despise thy words,
>   but thy word is joy and happiness to me,
> for thou hast named me thine, O LORD, God of hosts.

What has happened?

When Alexander the Great conquered most of the Middle East in the fourth century BCE, one of the lasting cultural results was the triumph of the Greek language as the common language (*koinē*) of the Empire. One of the products of this momentous change was a Greek translation of the Hebrew Bible, known to posterity as the Septuagint, which became the common Bible of the Greek-speaking

Jewish world for centuries. It is the Septuagint that Paul quotes from memory time and time again—and not always accurately—in his letters to the first Christian congregations. Very few Jews would have understood the ancient Hebrew of the original texts, and it is possible that the original Hebrew might have been incomprehensible to Paul himself.

The book of Jeremiah as it appears in the Septuagint sometimes differs strikingly from the Hebrew version that has come down to us in what is called the Masoretic text. The latter was compiled and edited by an extraordinary group of Jewish scholars, the Masoretes, who flourished from about 600 CE through the late tenth century. Modern editions of the Bible in Hebrew are still based on this Masoretic text. But the variant readings reflected in the Septuagint, as well as in other ancient versions in Aramaic, Syriac, and Latin, sometimes have as compelling a claim to authenticity as the Masoretic.

Although it is impossible to tell just from looking at the page of the 1970 NEB, a comparison between the Greek and Hebrew versions reveals that the translators of Jeremiah 15:16 might have based their work not on the Masoretic text, but on the Septuagint. They seem to have translated this Greek reading into what they think is its Hebrew equivalent, and then, with some additional conjectural emendations, translated this new text into English.[2] Although the translators adopted some of the Masoretic reading as well, in the end they arrive at a text and a translation that eliminates the striking metaphor that we find in the Hebrew ("Your words were found, and I ate them").

This is, of course, only one text out of many thousands, and only one editorial decision out of many thousands more. To an ordinary reader of Scripture, the details of such a decision can seem both overwhelming and pedantic. But small variants like this, multiplied a thousandfold in our own Bible editions, remind us how much we depend upon the work of linguists and text scholars as we encounter these ancient writings, and also how fluid and speculative some of these textual readings can be. Just as all translations are built on compromise, so are all critical editions of ancient texts themselves. At the very least, this fact should make us wary of taking too literal an attitude toward the Bible translations we read.

Many translations, including the NRSV itself, smooth out or eliminate challenging metaphors. Perhaps it was the jarring immediacy of Jeremiah's metaphor that prompted the original NEB translators to prefer the alternative text. It was a very small decision, but had it been preserved in the 1989 edition, now called the *Revised English Bible* (REB), that would have been a very great loss.

～ The Question of Inclusive Language

One feature that sets the NRSV translation apart from all other translations in the Tyndale tradition is its use of what has come to be called "inclusive language" in translating references to men and women in the Hebrew and Greek. Believing that the English language is by nature biased toward the masculine gender, so that English-language translations may restrict and obscure the original sense, the NRSV translators attempted to eliminate masculine language as much as they could without doing damage to the historical meaning of the text.

But the quest for inclusivity has also been taken further. In 1995 an editorial committee that included some of the original NRSV translators produced an unofficial revision of the NRSV that sought to extend the principles of inclusive language to the translation of words referring to God.

Thus, for example, the pronoun "him" or "he" is always avoided when referring to God, either by repeating the word "God," using another expression for God, or altering the syntax of the sentence to avoid the pronoun altogether. Arguing that the word "Father" as a title for God has by repetition lost its metaphorical power, and instead tends to be heard as if God were male, the editorial committee often translated the Greek word *Pater* simply as "God," and in several key passages of the New Testament translated the word with a new metaphor, "Father-Mother." Similarly, arguing rightly that the fact that Jesus was a man has no christological significance, the committee translated the word "Son" (Greek *huios*) as "Child," and the phrase "the Son of Man" (*huios anthrōpou*) as "the Human One." References to "the kingdom" (Greek *basilēus*) became "dominion"; celestial beings, whether angels or demons, were no longer given masculine pronouns. In the Psalter, the Hebrew word *Yahweh*, which you remember the NRSV translates as "the LORD," is rendered as "GOD," thereby avoiding what the committee saw as the unavoidably masculine connotations of the word "Lord."

Finally, the new version assiduously avoids language that would seem to imply that any kind of human disability characterizes someone's entire identity. Thus Matthew 11:5, which the NRSV translates as "the blind receive their sight, the lame walk, the lepers are cleansed, the deaf hear...and the poor have good news brought to them," has become "those who are blind receive their sight, those who are lame walk, the people with leprosy are cleansed, those who are deaf hear...and those who are poor have good news brought to them."[3]

It is much too early to say whether such a translation will catch on with ordinary Bible readers, or be used as one of the officially listed Bible translations approved by General Convention for public reading during divine worship. Like all versions and paraphrases, the new inclusive version can be instructive when used in comparison with other versions. But it must also be said that, in its own way, this version is as polemical and circular in its reasoning as its counterparts on the other end of the political and theological spectrum such as *The Living Bible*, in which the ancient text is also made to serve an ideological end. It may well be that the makers of the inclusive version attempt to do in translation what should really be done through teaching, preaching, and living example.

∼ Mining the Footnotes

Most of the time, annotated Bibles clearly indicate whether the editors have chosen from one of several possible versions of a particular verse or set of verses, and they will also indicate the manuscript sources for different possible readings. A mundane example is the matter-of-fact NOAB footnote to Jeremiah 16:7 informing us that the reading "No one shall break bread" is based on two Greek manuscripts: the Masoretic text (abbreviated MT) reads differently—"break for them." The editors chose what seemed to them the more coherent reading.

This concern to be forthright about the sometimes startling multiplicity of texts has a long and distinguished history, dating as far back as the Masoretes. Copying a manuscript of the Torah by hand was a painstaking process. It was also a religious act, prepared for by years of apprenticeship, and always accompanied by prayer. Because the consonantal text of the Hebrew Bible was sacred, editors and copiers of the manuscripts were loathe to correct occasional errors that had cropped up over centuries of copying. Instead, they devised a system of marginal annotation that preserved the inviolable integrity of the written text (in Aramaic, the *ketib*, "that which is written"), but offered the reader (who would more often than not be reading aloud) a corrected spelling or pronunciation (the *qere*, "that which is read aloud"). As the practice developed, it also gave scholars greater latitude. When there were two versions of an ancient text, each with a significant claim to precedence, this device allowed the scholars to offer both rather than choose between them.

Such details may seem excessive to a first-time Bible reader, and many of these textual variants are of interest only to scholars, but they do show us that the Bible is a *living* book. Although the Holy Scriptures "containeth all things necessary to salvation" (BCP 868), these writings did not arrive in a hermetically sealed box. The Bible is not a mute container of truth. It is a living creation, inspired by the living God, and the work of human hands in human communities—hands guided by the Holy Spirit through centuries of editing, translating, praying, copying, and rethinking, hands working across languages, across time, and across cultures. Reading the Bible takes energy—the energy produced by an open heart and mind, a critical eye, a willingness to listen, and the courage to allow our deepest convictions to be challenged, even our deepest convictions about the Bible itself.

Working with the translators' notes in an annotated Bible demonstrates that the shape of our inheritance is not always clear. That is the risk we take in participating in such an ancient tradition of reading: uncertainty simply goes with the territory. Even editors as conservative as the Masoretes recognized the need to take into account the anomalies and cross-purposes created by centuries of textual transmission. These too are part of our biblical heritage. All contemporary Bible editions reflect innumerable decisions about which ancient reading to incorporate into the standard text and which to relegate to footnotes. These decisions can raise compelling religious questions. Here are two examples of such questions, one drawn from the Hebrew Bible and one from the gospel of Mark.

"A virgin shall conceive..." (Isaiah 7:14)
One of the most familiar verses in the Old Testament is Isaiah 7:14, which reads like this in the *King James Version:*

> Therefore the Lord himself shall give you a sign; Behold, a virgin shall conceive, and bear a son, and shall call his name Immanuel.

Now compare it to the NRSV, which follows most contemporary translations:

> Therefore the Lord himself will give you a sign. Look, the young woman is with child and shall bear a son, and shall name him Immanuel.

Both editions provide a translator's note on the word "Immanuel," but the NRSV also offers a note on the phrase "young woman," which replaces the King James' "virgin."

The changes are slight, but theologically they are deeply significant. Both notes on "Immanuel," like many such notes in annotated editions of the Bible, offer the literal translation of a biblical name. Many names in the Hebrew scriptures are actually Hebrew phrases. When Jeremiah says "I am called by your name," part of what he means is that the name Jeremiah contains a form of the name of God in its last syllable. Often Hebrew names are symbolic, as in Isaiah 8, where we learn that the name *Maher-shalal-hash-baz* means "The spoil speeds, the prey hastens," a name designed to allay King Ahaz's panic before the coming battle. As the note for Isaiah 7:14 tells us (and as any lover

of Handel's *Messiah* will know immediately), Immanuel
means "God with us" (KJV) or "God is with us" (NRSV).

But for Christian readers through the centuries, who
have read the Hebrew Bible as a testament of prophecies
fulfilled in the gospels, this name Immanuel echoes with a
different kind of promise: the birth of Immanuel, the
Messiah, "God-with-us," from a virgin mother. Matthew's
gospel quotes this very passage in Isaiah to describe the
birth of Jesus:

> All this took place to fulfill what had been spoken by
> the Lord through the prophet:
>> "Look, the virgin shall conceive
>>> and bear a son,
>> and they shall name him
>>> Emmanuel,"
> which means, "God is with us." (Matthew 1:22-23)

This passage is so familiar to us as to seem unremarkable,
but it is in fact quite extraordinary. There are several
puzzles lurking. Why would the NRSV translators alter the
King James reading of "virgin" to "young woman" in their
translation of Isaiah 7:14, but then revert to the King James
usage when translating Matthew 1:23? And, for that matter, why should Matthew go to the trouble of translating
the word "Emmanuel," when any Jewish reader would
know immediately what it meant?

The answers to these questions are a little complicated,
but they reveal a lot about what the Bible is and what it is
not. Here is the note that the NRSV offers for "young
woman": "Gk *the virgin*." Behind this stark note lurk generations of theological controversy. "Virgin," of course, was
the translation employed by the King James translators, as
well as other translators before them. But they were following an interpretation of the Hebrew text found in the

Greek Septuagint, where the Hebrew *'almah,* "young woman," is translated by the Greek word *parthenos,* "maiden, virgin." The NRSV translators prefer the Masoretic text instead, assuming (and rightly so) that the Greek is less reliable, since it is a relatively late translation of the original Hebrew. Furthermore, in a longer note appearing below the main text, the annotators provide other occurrences of *'almah* in the Hebrew Bible, where it is variously translated as "young woman" or "girl." In the light of such data the NRSV translators thought it best to give the word *'almah* the meaning it seems to have had in Old Testament times.

It is from small technical decisions like this that large theological controversies arise. Since New Testament times, Christians have understood this prophecy in Isaiah to be a prediction of the Messiah's birth from a virgin. The NRSV translators undercut this traditional reading, not because they do not believe in the teachings about the virgin birth (they might or they might not), but because they seek the utmost accuracy in rendering the Hebrew text before them. The translators arrive at their decision on sound scholarly principles and tell us their reason in the notes.

And in this case they are in good company. The Roman Catholic translators of the *Jerusalem Bible,* who have just as great a stake in the doctrine of the virgin birth, also prefer the Hebrew reading to the Greek. In their note, the Roman Catholic translators take pains to point out that the Greek reading, while not the word used originally in the Hebrew text, may be nonetheless an important witness to a later tradition, which tells of a virgin birth of a hero-Savior. The editors quietly speculate that such a tradition was extant at the time the Septuagint translators were at work. Knowledge of such a tradition would have increased the likelihood that the Greek-speaking Jewish translators, working hundreds of years before Christ's birth, would choose the Greek word *parthenos* to translate the Hebrew word *'almah*. Thus the young woman of Isaiah becomes the virgin of the Septuagint.

Which brings us back to Matthew's nativity story. Like most first-century Jews, the writer of Matthew's gospel would have been working from the Greek text of Isaiah as he composed his gospel. Matthew wrote in Greek for a Greek-speaking audience, many of whom had a Jewish background, some of whom probably knew Aramaic but not biblical Hebrew. Hebrew would have been as much a mystery to most first-century Jews as church Latin was to most twentieth-century Roman Catholics. So Matthew translated the word "Immanuel" in the course of his text (no one had recourse to footnotes in those days), for the benefit of his non-Hebrew speaking listeners and readers. Two millennia later, translating Matthew's gospel into English, the NRSV translators adhere strictly to Matthew's Greek text, where the word *parthenos* appears. In the translation of Isaiah 7:14 the NRSV employs another English word in an attempt to give a more accurate rendition of the original oracle of Isaiah.

As you can see, if you have patience enough to pursue them, translators' footnotes and commentaries can reveal much not only about the history of the Bible itself, but also about the presuppositions, desires, and longings of the various communities which the biblical traditions have shaped, including our own. To read Scripture with an ear to its own history is to begin to overhear centuries of conversation about texts that matter deeply to people, and to be invited to participate in those conversations yourself. And as with all conversations, the more you know, the more intelligently you can participate. Knowing the history of these famous passages in the Hebrew Bible and the New

Testament doesn't mean that you have to abandon the doctrine of the virgin birth—far from it. But such knowledge does challenge you to reconsider the grounds on which you hold it.

"...for they were afraid" (Mark 16:8)

Another key text in the development of the Christian proclamation is the story of Jesus' resurrection and the account of the empty tomb as found in Mark. The story is told in each of the four gospels, but Mark's is the shortest and most abrupt. Most New Testament scholars think that the accounts in Matthew and Luke depend on Mark's, while John's account reflects an independent tradition. By overwhelming consensus Mark is also thought to be the first gospel to be written, probably around the year 70 CE, almost forty years after the occurrence of the events it records. Given Mark's importance chronologically in the development of the New Testament writings, the abrupt ending of his gospel has drawn considerable attention over the centuries, especially in recent decades. The fact is, the situation is quite messy, as even a glance at the annotated page will tell you: you will find a lot of commentary surrounding a small amount of text. In reading the Bible, encountering such lavish commentary is often a clue that something important is afoot.

We need to be aware in approaching a passage like this that many manuscripts and fragments of manuscripts recording Mark's gospel have survived to our own day. As with the manuscripts of the Hebrew Bible, most of these were produced centuries after the gospel was first written, being copies of copies of copies of one or another version of the lost original. Unlike the Hebrew Bible, however, which was written and edited over the course of a millennium, the New Testament was produced in the relatively short span of a hundred years that are recent enough for fragments of a significant number of the earliest manuscripts to have survived. Scholars over many generations have devised protocols and hierarchies for sorting through this vast, confusing cache of material, taking into account everything from the style of handwriting to the carbon-14 dating of the papyrus. Working with such material is exceedingly tricky. For example, sometimes a manuscript dating from a later century will be found on stylistic grounds to reflect a more accurate source than a manuscript dated earlier but based on less reliable sources. Text scholars have spent lifetimes debating such questions, and without the difficult decisions they make about what reading is authentic and what is not, it would be impossible for us to read our Bibles with any confidence at all.

Of the many puzzles posed by the New Testament manuscripts, the ending of Mark's gospel is one of the most difficult and provocative. In effect, there are not one but three endings (perhaps even four) extant in the manuscripts. First there is the abrupt ending at 16:8:

> So they went out and fled from the tomb, for terror and amazement had seized them; and they said nothing to anyone, for they were afraid.

Since ancient times, readers of the Greek text have remarked on the oddity of this last sentence because of the fact that the last clause ends with a weak word, the particle *gar* ("for"). While clauses having the same structure as "for they were afraid" can be found in a few other Greek texts, such usage is far from usual. To a number of distinguished readers, both ancient and modern, this seems no way to end a gospel.[4]

Even readers who have no knowledge of Greek find the passage jarring. In the gospel accounts of Matthew and

Luke, we are told that the women run to tell the good news of the resurrection to Peter and the other disciples. The tone is joyful, full of anticipation and triumph. In John's moving story of Mary Magdalene's encounter with the risen Jesus, the tone is characteristically poignant and calm. Mark's gospel has none of this. The women greet the news of the resurrection not with joy but with terror. They do not hurry to spread the news. Instead they flee, afraid for their sanity and for their reputation, deserting the empty tomb as precipitately as the disciples deserted Jesus at his arrest.

Over the centuries, readers have offered many explanations for this strange and counterintuitive ending. Some of these explanations can be amusing: Mark died suddenly after writing 16:8, or perhaps the last page of the manuscript fell off. In a classic essay, the distinguished literary critic Frank Kermode argues cogently that passages like this in the Bible do not sit well with readers seeking closure and fulfillment, what Kermode calls elsewhere "the sense of an ending."[5] If he is right, no wonder that additional endings to Mark's gospel have cropped up in the tradition. One ancient authority provides what the Oxford annotators call "the shorter ending," a single verse that attempts in one remarkable sentence to make up for all that seems to be missing. It has the women "briefly" tell the people around Peter what they had seen, and then ends the gospel on an upbeat note, with "the sacred and imperishable proclamation of eternal salvation." For double emphasis, a few of the ancient authorities add the word *Amen*.

But most of the ancient sources that want to improve Mark's ending use what the annotators call "the longer ending," which provides the kind of post-resurrection appearances we find at the end of the other three gospels. They include an intriguing mention of Mary Magdalene ("from whom he had cast out seven demons"), as well as a remarkable passage about picking up snakes and drinking poison, activities without precedent in any of the other New Testament writings. Finally, on the last page of the Oxford Annotated's version of Mark, we find yet another ending. This one has been relegated completely to a translator's note and features apocalyptic imagery that may reflect the anxieties of a succeeding generation of Christians suffering under persecution:

> Christ replied to them, "The term of years of Satan's power has been fulfilled, but other terrible things draw near. And for those who have sinned I was handed over to death, that they may return to the truth and sin no more, that they may inherit the spiritual and imperishable glory of righteousness that is in heaven." (Mark 16:14, note *t*)

On balance, none of these endings is very persuasive. Important witnesses, including some of the most ancient authorities, end the gospel at 16:8, and the stylistic differences distinguishing the "longer ending" from the rest of Mark's gospel make it next to impossible to argue that these additional verses were a part of Mark's original text. If the writer of Mark 16:8 wrote more than we have here, it has not survived. If he didn't, then somehow we have to come to terms with an ending that doesn't seem like an ending.

We all make our separate peace with puzzles like this in reading the Bible. Since a compelling case can be made that the earliest text ends with Mark 16:8, what can we do with the abruptness and inconclusiveness of that last sentence? I actually find the inconclusiveness of Mark's ending attractive. Like many of Jesus' parables, Mark's ending does not tell us "what happened afterward." Instead, we find ourselves challenged to come to terms with our own presuppositions about life and death, our own fears, and our own imaginings. As interesting as these texts are to historians, we are not reading history here, or at least not the kind of history that most of us are used to. To read Mark's story of the resurrection is to prepare yourself to be challenged by this news, to share the fear and terror of the women who flee, and to decide afterwards, as the women must decide, whether you can stay the course once the full story is known. Reading Mark's gospel invites you to an act of faith—to come to believe, or to continue to believe. Like the ending of Mark's gospel, it is an invitation that is always open. After all, open endings and open invitations are what gospels are all about.

Chapter 5

Interpreting the Explanatory Notes

> ...bless those who curse you, pray for those who abuse you. (Luke 6:28)
>
> **28:** Luke's Jesus gives the greatest example of this on the cross, if the verse is authentic.... *(NOAB explanatory note)*

Reading explanatory notes like this one in an annotated Bible can be both informative and frustrating. Who decides what is said and what is not, or which Scripture verses are authentic and which are not? How can we be sure that the perspectives and biases of the annotators haven't crept into the text itself? Why don't the notes explain more than they do? For that matter, why bother with notes at all? Doesn't the Bible speak plainly and clearly enough by itself? These questions have a history closely tied to the history of the Anglican Church in Reformation England and, by extension, to the Episcopal Church today. But the story starts long before the sixteenth century.

~ Jewish Talmud and Christian Gloss

Combining sacred text and commentary on a single page is a very old tradition for both Jews and Christians. By tradition, the great Torah scrolls read aloud in synagogues contain no written commentary, but apart from these solemn occasions of synagogue reading, the need for commentary has always been strong. About the time that the Christian Bible was beginning to take shape in the first and second centuries, what Jewish tradition calls the Oral Law began to be recorded in writing, known collectively as the Talmud. All rabbis today—Orthodox, Conservative, and Reform—are trained in Talmudic studies. In the most orthodox Jewish circles, the daily study of the Talmud commentaries functions as an anchor of community life.

This vast compendium of law, story, and commentary, written in a difficult mixture of Hebrew and Aramaic, has come down to us not on scrolls but in the more convenient codex form, each page of which over the centuries developed a daunting visual complexity. A page of the Talmud displays a postcard-size rectangle of Aramaic text at the center. It contains a section of the *Mishnah*, the oldest commentary on the Torah, accompanied by a section of the *Gemara*, in turn the oldest commentary on the Mishnah. The Mishnah and Gemara are surrounded by several other commentaries dating from later periods.

The page breathes its history. To read Talmud in a traditional setting—under the leadership of a rabbi and in the company of other readers with varying degrees of sophistication and expertise—is to learn to negotiate several conversations at once, conversations taking place across the centuries. The reader takes in this "virtual" conversation recorded on the page surrounding the Talmud text, and at the same time participates in the conversations of the other Talmud readers at the table as well. The conversation includes many voices: the voice of the Talmud passage itself, the Torah passage on which it comments, the commentaries on the Talmud surrounding the original passage at the center of the page, the observations of the rabbi leading the discussion, and the students surrounding the rabbi at the table.

Jonathan Boyarin, an anthropologist who studies the ethnography of reading, once joined a Talmud class in a small, struggling *yeshiva* on the lower East Side of New York City to observe these complex interactions. There he discovered a powerful example of sacred reading in dialogue, as the holy texts were transformed and made contemporary by the playful dialogue between teacher, text, and student. Their playfulness was grounded in turn by the seriousness of the tradition that text, teacher, and student together both respected and embodied. Tradition in the *yeshiva*, Boyarin concluded, was not a dead weight from the past but a living process, dynamic and dialectic. Text and speech were of equal priority: "The task of Jewish study is to create community among Jews through time via language."[1] And that community found its model in the structure of the Talmud page itself, with its many voices.

The Yiddish word for this shared reading is *lernen*, a word that applies whether you are a seasoned scholar or a recently bar-mitzvahed neophyte. It is a process both tremendously playful, full of puns and inside jokes, and deeply earnest. Such playfulness would strike many Christian Bible readers as inappropriate and bizarre, even a little blasphemous, but it is none of these things. For an observant Jew, the reading of Scripture is a shared experience, and at root it is a joyous one. In the words of the very first psalm: "Their delight is in the law of the LORD,/ and on his law they meditate day and night" (Psalm 1:2). *Lernen* is an activity deeply woven into the fabric of everyday life. And there is no end to it, for once the vast material of the Talmud has been traversed—a process that takes many years—the game begins again. For over a thousand years, this collaborative act of reading the Talmud has been the essential religious activity for generations of Orthodox and Hasidic Jewish men—and now, in more progressive circles, of women too.

For many reasons, Christians have had a harder time of it. Over the centuries, Christian traditions of reading have been more various and fragmented, and considerably more contested. Particularly after the Reformation, Christian traditions of reading became less playful, and often much more individualistic and isolating, than traditional Jewish *lernen*. But it was not always so. In the Middle Ages there was a Christian counterpart to the Talmud page in widespread use, the heavily annotated Latin Bible known as the *Glossa ordinaria*, or simply the *Glossa*. Written in Latin, it contained commentaries on St. Jerome's fourth-century translation of the Bible known as the Vulgate, the official translation for Roman Catholics until well into modern times. In Catholic Europe, generally speaking, this Latin Bible was the only Bible; Hebrew and Greek were known only to a very few. Difficult to use without years of training, the glossed Latin Bible was intended for clergy and scholars. Although the books were extremely elaborate to make, there were many copies in circulation, though their readership was restricted to men (and some women) well-versed in the Latin culture of the monasteries and the cathedral schools. Most of the rest of the population of Europe was illiterate; they experienced their Bibles aurally and visually—by hearing sermons and homilies, by participating in the dynamic street theater of the mystery plays, and by meditating on the biblical images portrayed in the stone carvings and stained-glass windows that were the glory of the cathedral and abbey churches. These images constituted the common Bible of the people. To the majority of Christian Europe, the *Glossa* itself was a closed book.

How did the page look to someone who could read it? Like the Talmud, a typical page exhibited an amazing complexity. In its more sumptuous illuminated form, it could be an object of great beauty. The principal text for discussion—always a passage from Jerome's Vulgate— usually occupied a privileged position near the center of the large folio page, while the rest of the page was packed with the accumulated commentaries of centuries, running along the margins and interspersed between the lines. These included a representative selection of extracts from the church fathers and other theologians from the third to the early twelfth century, and functioned in the same way as the rabbinical commentaries around the borders of the Talmud page.[2] In fact, some of the later commentary in the Christian *Glossa* was influenced by the same rabbis who compiled and contributed to the Talmud, particularly the great medieval rabbi known as Rashi.

As with the Talmud, no one person can be credited with assembling the *Glossa*. It took centuries to accumulate its contents, reflecting the contributions of a wide number of intellectual schools. The glossed Latin Bible offered commentary sanctioned by institutional consensus. If the Bible were to be read properly in the Middle Ages, its interpretation would be governed by the content and the methods of these official commentaries on this official page.

The fourfold method

Rooted in the writings of Paul and in the work of early interpreters like Origen and Augustine, but developed over many centuries, one of the *Glossa*'s central features was what is often called the fourfold reading of Scripture. Like the great medieval cathedrals, and the ordered cosmologies their architecture sought to reflect, the biblical text shimmered with layers of meaning for the medieval reader. What the text actually says, including the historical event it describes, is its primary or "literal" sense. But for the medieval reader trained to discern them, there are other senses as well—the allegorical, the moral, and the mystical. Together these contribute to what the great thirteenth-century theologian Thomas Aquinas called the *sensus spiritualis*, or spiritual sense of the words on the page and the events they report. The spiritual sense invites the reader to recognize in one event an allegorical type or foreshadowing of another. The word "allegory" comes from Greek words for "reading" and "other," so to read allegorically is to "read otherwise." At the same time, one could discern a moral (or "tropological") meaning as well as an "anagogical" or mystical, one that revealed the mysteries of the Last Things and the Heavenly Jerusalem.

One of the most sensitive and brilliant practitioners of this art was the Florentine poet Dante Alighieri, whose *Divine Comedy* creates from this allegorical sensibility an epic poem of consummate beauty. In a letter to his friend and patron, Can Grande della Scala, Dante himself gives a characteristic reading of Psalm 114:

> When Israel went out from Egypt,
>   the house of Jacob from a people of strange language,
> Judah became God's sanctuary,
>   Israel his dominion. (Psalm 114:1-2)

"If we look to the letter alone," Dante writes,

> the departure of the children of Israel from Egypt in the time of Moses is indicated to us; if to the allegory, our

redemption accomplished by Christ;...if to the moral sense, the conversion of the soul from the woe and misery of sin to a state of grace;...if to the anagogical sense, the departure of the consecrated soul from the slavery of this corruption to the liberty of eternal glory.[3]

In the opening scene of the *Purgatorio*, the second part of the *Divine Comedy*, Dante embodies this "spiritual" approach to the Bible in the drama of his poem. Fresh from the horrific visions of his sojourn in hell, Dante the pilgrim awakes to find himself on the shore of a wide sea at the foot of the purgatorial mountain he must ascend. In the distance he hears the sound of chanting coming faintly toward him from across the sea, and soon discovers that it is Psalm 114 he hears, sung by the souls of the redeemed as they approach: "*In exitu Israel de Aegypto...*, 'When Israel came out of Egypt,' all of them were singing together with one voice, with the rest of that psalm that is written."[4] Although the poem itself is written in Italian, Dante reproduces the Latin text of the psalm exactly as it appears in the Vulgate. Faithful to the "letter" of Scripture, at the same time he allows its spiritual sense to shape the purgatorial drama. It is a moment of tremendous human pathos, mixed with sadness, calmness, and hope. As Israel once crossed the Red Sea (the literal sense), so the saved souls traverse the Great Sea (the allegorical sense). Saved in the waters of baptism for this time of trial and purgation (the moral or tropological sense), they make their way up the purgatorial mountain toward the Earthly Paradise and the Heavenly Jerusalem (the mystical or anagogical sense).

The numerous variations on the fourfold method of reading that animated Dante's great epic were ultimately given institutional form in the pages of the *Glossa*. At its best, the method could provide medieval readers like Dante with imaginative and interpretive tools of great subtlety, creating a powerful means of access to sometimes challenging biblical texts. But not everyone could be as sensitive a practitioner of this method as Aquinas or Dante. The danger was an overreading that could swamp the literal sense, resulting not in shimmering hierarchies of meaning but vast superstructures of allegory that crushed the original text under their weight. The method sometimes seduced overzealous interpreters into elaborate and overcharged readings that seemed to abandon the "letter" of Scripture altogether. In the eyes of the Protestant reformers of the sixteenth century, the pages of the *Glossa* made the reading of Scripture seem like the exclusive province of a privileged caste trained to plumb its elusive mysteries. By the time it appeared in print, the glossed Bible with its allegorizing commentary had become all but standardized in the Latin church. Like Dante's *Divine Comedy*, but without its imaginative vision, the *Glossa* was a monument to the homogenous monastic and scholastic intellectual culture of the late Middle Ages.

～ William Tyndale and "Simple Plain Sense"

Even before King Henry VIII dissolved the monasteries in England in the 1520s, dispersing the monks and nuns and seizing their land and treasures, the shared cultural values uniting the monasteries and schools that produced the *Glossa* had themselves begun to dissolve. In a time when Renaissance humanists like Erasmus were rediscovering the value of working directly with the Hebrew and Greek texts, and when Luther and his followers were urging regular Bible reading on all Christian people, the *Glossa*'s elaborate and forbidding style of commentary came under considerable fire. During the English Reformation the *Glossa* itself became a symbol for the institutional power of the Roman Church to coerce readers to accept a single point of view about the meaning of Scripture:

> They divide the scripture into four senses, the literal, the tropological, allegorical, and anagogical. The literal sense is become nothing at all: for the pope hath taken it clean away, and hath made it his possession. He hath partly locked it up with the false and counterfeited keys of his traditions, ceremonies, and feigned lies; for no man dare abide by the literal sense of the text, but under a protestation, "if it please the pope."[5]

The sharp-tongued critic who wrote these words was William Tyndale, whose English translation of the entire New Testament and half of the Old in the 1520s and 1530s became the model for all English translations to follow. Tyndale was convinced that the text of the Bible was plain for all to understand—it had a "simple literal sense." He fiercely rejected the elaborate allegorical scheme of the *Glossa* together with the powerful institution that would foist these interpretations on the plain-spoken, plain-seeing reader. The commentators "wrest" Scripture to their own purposes, Tyndale wrote in his *Obedience of a Christian Man*, "clean contrary" to the meaning of the text. Tyndale's mockery is ruthless; these commentators delude the reader by "descanting on the text" with allegories, and amuse themselves by "expounding it in many senses before the unlearned lay people (when it hath but one simple literal sense whose light the owls can not abide)."

The appearance of the page in his own printed editions (no columns, few annotations) reflects Tyndale's conviction that Scripture could speak plainly and unadorned. His plain-speaking was risky: he produced these pages under conditions of considerable personal danger. In a raw display of the very institutional power that Tyndale spent such energy criticizing, an agent of the English king betrayed Tyndale in Antwerp to the police of the Catholic emperor. He was strangled and burned at the stake in 1536, just as his books had been burned, all this only a few months before Henry VIII himself would authorize the printing of an English Bible inspired by Tyndale's principles.

Small enough to hold (or hide) in the hand, Tyndale's English translation of 1526 appears in page-wide format, without columns or verse numbering. The comments he includes in the prefaces, chapter summaries, and occasional notes of later editions are in content and tone worlds removed from the pages of the medieval *Glossa*. Tyndale's comments "rarely explicate and never allegorize the text; rather, they draw parallels (or, more often, contrasts) between the biblical texts and the present state of the church."[6] Some of these parallels were notorious, winning him many powerful enemies; ironically, Tyndale's own glossing probably cost him his life. A famous example is his comment on Leviticus 10:8, where God tells Aaron to drink no wine. Unlike sober Aaron, Tyndale notes, "our prelates be drunk with desire of honor and have brought the world out of their wits to satisfy their lusts, and live not soberly to teach us what Christ commanded by the hands of the apostles."

Nevertheless, Tyndale's views on the plainness of Scripture and his confidence in the ability of ordinary readers to understand it helped transform Anglican attitudes toward Bible reading. His indomitable spirit empowered even the most intimidated of readers to open the sacred page and read for themselves. One of the most widely read books in Reformation England and later in colonial America was John Foxe's *Acts and Monuments of Matters Happening in the Church*, known familiarly as Foxe's *Book of Martyrs*. In one of its more memorable passages, Foxe quotes Tyndale's fighting words to a skeptical "learned man" who had claimed "we were better to be without God's laws than the pope's": "I defy the Pope and all his laws. If God spare my life, ere many years I will cause a boy that driveth the plough should know more of scripture than thou dost."[7]

But Tyndale and his successors also provided the innocent plowboy with commentary to guide him. Almost every English Bible printed in the century after Tyndale's featured some form of explanatory and interpretive material, often much more contentious than his. In the several English versions that appeared between Tyndale's day and the year the King James translation was published, 1611, the margins around the text and the space below became hotly contested battlegrounds. Some Bibles officially sanctioned by the Crown featured pictures of a pointing hand in the margin, warning readers off from certain passages; another, produced by British Catholics living in exile in France following the death of the Catholic Queen Mary in 1558, pointedly used the Vulgate text used in the *Glossa* as the basis for translation. (The Latin text remained the only authorized version of the Bible for use in translation in the Roman Church until well into this century.) The compilers of this Catholic translation, named the *Douai-Rheims*, stood firm against the uncertainties of interpretation created by a return to the original Greek and Hebrew texts, and against the Protestant rejection of Roman authority. But by the late 1570s, the most popular Bible in England was the new translation first published in 1560 by the English Protestants in Geneva. With its innovative typography, copious introductions, charts, maps, and explanatory notes, it was the most user-friendly Bible in print. Its commentary was also the most Protestant and radical, criticizing not only the power of the pope but also (at least by implication) the power of the Crown as well.

Like the Reformation monarchs who preceded him, James I was no radical. When he commissioned a new translation of the Bible in the early 1600s, he acted decisively to eliminate the sometimes "bitter" marginal notes of the Geneva Bible. Two of the notes he took personally were on Exodus 1:19, which defends disobedience to kings, and 2 Chronicles 15:15, which criticizes King Asa for deposing his mother from the throne rather than executing her. When you remember that James's own mother was Mary, Queen of Scots, executed by her cousin Elizabeth when James was a child, you get a sense of how much was at stake for the Crown in authorizing commentaries and controlling what they said. It is no accident that radical dissenters like the Pilgrims carried the subversive Geneva Bible with them when they emigrated to America, where it was the favored Bible of the new American colonies, and not the King James.

Although in the United States there is no longer a monarch who makes decrees about these matters, the Episcopal Church still exercises considerable caution today when it decides which Bible translations it will recognize as authoritative and acceptable for use in public worship. But listing officially recognized translations is as far as church jurisdiction can go. Personal study Bibles are a different matter. For purposes of study and discussion, Episcopalians have never recognized a central teaching authority like the Roman Catholic magisterium that controls the boundaries of debate. There is no final arbiter of disputed interpretations. As a result, Episcopalians as individuals are free to use whatever annotated editions of the Bible appeal to them (and preferably several), guided only by the broad general outlines of creed and prayer book. In modern Anglican practice the spirit of Tyndale and the English exiles in Geneva lives on.

Paradoxically, even though Episcopalians pride themselves on the freedom and diverse points of view that they bring to the interpretation of the Bible, it is the more conservative traditions of commentary that are immediately evident in the annotated Bibles they use the most. In their terse notes, in their careful attention to text and translation, and even in the layout of their pages, most annotated Bibles in English (including Roman Catholic ones) reflect the same measured, humanistic, and conservative principles that lay behind the so-called authorized version of King James I. These Bible editions display a firm confidence in the reader's ability both to read the sacred text with intelligence and to use the annotations with discretion. Their annotators act with discretion themselves, keeping the commentary below the bar-line to a minimum. Their task is to explain, but not to interpret or to preach.

It is fitting that such Bibles should appeal to present-day Episcopalians, for ours is a double legacy. Episcopalians inherit the Reformation freedom to read and interpret Scripture for themselves, but we do so informed by two thousand years of catholic tradition, by the exercise of historical and critical thinking, and by the resources of our own human experience. Using an annotated Bible like the Oxford grounds us in the insights of the past as we interpret these texts for the present. At a minimum, the notes keep us honest. Only after we understand what the text meant in its own day can we begin to fathom its meaning for ours. Good annotations make us continually answerable to the wider community of readers of which we form a part—a community of believers united by the Spirit who inspired these texts and who dwells among its interpreters. And as

the notes frequently demonstrate, being united in the Spirit
is no guarantee that all readers' voices will agree.

~ Tracing Cross-References

> 46   And Mary said,
>   "My soul magnifies the Lord,
> 47   and my spirit rejoices in God my Savior,
> 48   for he has looked with favor on
>   the lowliness of his servant. (Luke 1:46–48)
> **1.46-55** The "Magnificat" (so called from the first word
> of the Latin translation) is based largely on Hannah's
> prayer in 1 Sam 2.1-10. *(NOAB explanatory note)*

Cross-references like this one are the backbone of annotated
Bibles. Hearing the Magnificat as Luke presents it is wonderful; but it is even better with Hannah's great song of
praise in 1 Samuel echoing in the ear. We suddenly gain
access to the evangelist's imagination, who told the story
of Mary and the angel knowing full well that it reflected
the earlier story. Luke probably had the song of Hannah in
mind when he wrote about Mary. We later readers have to
depend on the kindness of annotators to remind us how to
listen for these echoes.

Such listening is more easily described than accomplished. Given the thousands of cross-references that are
cited in annotated Bibles, chasing down every one can be
time-consuming. But following up even a few can be
exhilarating. Using these invaluable tools, readers can in
effect construct their own commentaries on the Bible. No
wonder that voluminous cross-referencing was one of the
most prominent features of Reformation Bibles, made possible by the meticulous numbering of chapter and verse
that had developed in the first few generations of printing.
The English reformers sought to train Christians to read

the Bible on their own. The Bible was accessible to all, even in its most obscure places. They believed that no text in the Bible was so obscure that it could not be illuminated by another passage elsewhere. As one Elizabethan preacher said: "Although many things in the Scripture be spoken in obscure mysteries, yet there is no thing spoken under dark mysteries in one place, but the self same thing in other places is spoken more familiarly and plainly, to the capacity both of learned and unlearned."[8]

This preacher's confidence in the Bible's ability to explain itself echoes sentiments dating at least as far back as Augustine in the fourth century. It also is in the spirit of ancient Jewish traditions of reading Scripture, embodied in the New Testament writings, the Talmud, the *midrashim,* and in medieval Jewish mystic writings like the *Zohar.* In our day, this confidence is reflected in the construction of the eucharistic lectionaries in the prayer books of the liturgical churches, where readings from the Old Testament and the New Testament epistles are often chosen for the light they shed on the gospel readings that follow them. In other words, in the Anglican tradition the best way to read the Bible is to read it *with* and *through* the Bible. Following up cross-references allows you to watch the Bible in effect reading and commenting on itself—a conversation in which the reader is expected to participate.

Cross-references can also illuminate the process by which some parts of the Bible came to be. As the collection of writings constituting the Hebrew Bible developed and grew, later writers revisited the ancient texts and reshaped them to speak to present circumstances. The book of Deuteronomy, a book crucial to the reform of the kingdom of Judah in the days of King Josiah, retells and reshapes materials found in earlier books of the Torah in order to speak to the conditions of an Israel under duress. So too the late books of Chronicles retell and reshape materials found in the much more expansive books of 1 and 2 Samuel and 1 and 2 Kings. These later versions are not so much revisions as re-visionings, and annotated Bibles help us to notice them.

The ways that this reading of Scripture creates new Scripture are particularly striking in the New Testament. We have already seen how the writer of the book of Revelation could recall and then reimagine the powerful scroll metaphors in Jeremiah and Ezekiel. Large sections of the New Testament quote or reshape the Old Testament writings, sometimes in startling ways. The gospel writers saw key events in Jesus' life foreshadowed in the writings of the Hebrew Bible, just as Paul's letters frequently engage in this "typological" reading and extend it to key liturgical events in the life of his congregations. Paul presents baptism, for example, in the language of the Exodus, and understands Christ's sacrifice as repeating and replacing the sacrifice of the paschal lamb described in Leviticus. Paul was a confirmed practitioner of allegorical and typological methods, shaped by his own training as a Pharisee in the sometimes wildly creative strategies of *midrash* and *pesher.* The same is true for all the New Testament writers. Every time we hear Matthew tell us that something has happened "so that the Scripture might be fulfilled" or watch the author of the letter to the Hebrews construct an elaborate theology of Christ as High Priest and paschal victim, we hear and see the Bible reading itself. The elaborate typologies and allegories devised by the medieval Bible readers had deep biblical precedent.

No set of cross-references is exhaustive, however, and the cross-references that editors choose to make can be theologically revealing. Take the Oxford note to Jeremiah 16:1-4, where Jeremiah is prevented from taking a wife.

The Oxford cross-reference suggests that the reader compare a passage in 1 Corinthians, where Paul describes the unmarried state in similar prophetic terms. Paul often describes his call as an apostle in language associated with the call of prophets like Jeremiah, and these two passages both exhibit the urgency of the prophetic conviction that the end of time is at hand. Anyone interested in Paul's writings would appreciate the cross-reference in the note.

But such cross-referencing between the Old and the New Testament might well be puzzling, even offensive, to a Jewish reader of Jeremiah. From a Jewish point of view, the passage in Paul may be of historical interest, but it sheds no light at all on the meaning of the passage in Jeremiah in and of itself. Cross-references like this are clearly intended for a Christian readership. The Oxford annotators are temperate and low-key in presenting their Christian point of view, but others can be less accommodating. Historically, cross-references connecting the Old Testament with the New have served sometimes bitterly argumentative ends, especially in Bibles like the *Scofield Reference Bible*, whose editors hold that the New Testament has "superseded" the Old. Supersessionist theology has been the hallmark of Christian attitudes toward Hebrew Scripture since earliest Christian times; in recent years, both the Roman Catholic Church and the Episcopal Church have pulled away from such extreme positions, insisting that the Hebrew Bible retains its own integrity no matter how the New Testament writers or later Christians have sought to appropriate and reinterpret it. It is well to keep this history in mind as you follow cross-references connecting the two parts of the Christian Bible.

Prominent in the Oxford New Testament notes are cross-references to parallel passages in the four gospels—Matthew, Mark, Luke, and John. Comparing the sometimes striking differences among the gospel accounts is essential to understanding the variety of narrative strategies and theological perspectives that distinguish one evangelist from the other. The Oxford cites parallels in the first note to each new episode of a gospel; for example, it tells us that Mark's account of the empty tomb is paralleled in Matthew 28, Luke 24, and John 20. More specific parallels occur as well; the note to Mark 16:8 suggests we compare the troubling silence of the women as Mark describes it to the contrasting mood of the passages in Matthew and Luke.

In the history of New Testament research, the careful study of gospel parallels like these has been instrumental in furthering the so-called quest for the historical Jesus. For most of this century, scholars have assumed that material found in Matthew and Luke but not in Mark indicates that the first two share a source unknown to Mark: a lost "document" or oral tradition known as Q, from the German word *Quelle*, meaning "source." Speculation about the nature of Q has dovetailed in recent years with research into other gospels outside the New Testament canon, like the gospel of Thomas, found among the library of manuscripts buried in the desert sands near Nag Hammadi. Even for the nonspecialist, tracing the differences among parallel gospel accounts, including the gospel of Thomas, can help to uncover the extraordinary variety of ways the earliest believers sought to tell the story of their encounter with the risen Jesus.

∽ Explaining Difficult Passages

3   But I want you to understand that Christ is the head of every man, and the husband is the head of his wife, and God is the head of Christ.   4   Any man who prays or prophesies with something on his head disgraces his

head, 5 but any woman who prays or prophesies
with her head unveiled disgraces her head—it is one and
the same thing as having her head shaved. (1 Corinthians 11:3-5)

11.3-5 A play on the word *head*: v. 3, "source," see v.
8; 15.28, but in 4a (and 5-7) a physical sense, and 4b
his head and *her head* may denote Christ. Reflecting
first-century culture, a man dishonors Christ by worshiping with his head covered; a woman dishonors both
her husband and Christ by worshiping otherwise.
(NOAB explanatory note)

The need to explain difficult passages or obscure words is
almost as old as Scripture. Even Paul's near-contemporaries
had problems. A late first-century biblical writer tells us
that there are some things in Paul's letters that are "hard
to understand, which the ignorant and the unstable twist
to their own destruction, as they do the other scriptures"
(2 Peter 3:15-16). When we latter-day readers of Paul find
ourselves perplexed (and perhaps put off) by passages like
the one just cited from 1 Corinthians, we can take some
comfort from the fact that we are not the first people to
feel that way.

In fact, the Bible is so ancient and varied an anthology
of texts that it is sometimes forced to comment on itself.
We have already seen how the writer of Matthew's gospel
needed to translate the word "Immanuel" for a Greek-
speaking audience to whom the Hebrew word would have
been a mystery. In the Hebrew Bible, writers of later texts
sometimes need to elucidate or explain earlier texts that
they are quoting or adapting. This is even more striking in
the New Testament, written at a time when people speaking
several different languages and holding to different customs found themselves living in close quarters in the midst

of crowded trade routes. The clash of cultures often led to mutual puzzlement and considerable animosity. The three languages that Pilate orders his cohorts to use in the mocking placard posted on Jesus' cross testify to the multilingualism of that time and place (see John 19:16-22). Frequently an Aramaic phrase or place-name like Golgotha, which the writer of John's gospel describes as a word "in Hebrew" for the benefit of his Greek-speaking audience, needs translation or comment. Jesus' words from the cross in Mark quote the Aramaic version of Psalm 22 (*Eloi, Eloi, lama sabbacthani*, "My God, my God, why have you forsaken me?") and are then translated by the evangelist into Greek (Mark 15:34).

Today we can add to the Bible's inner commentary the insights and discoveries of many generations of scholars—linguists, archeologists, historians, liturgists, anthropologists, sociologists, text editors, and literary critics. Good annotated editions of the Bible take advantage of their work, putting modern-day Episcopalians in a much better position to read with understanding than their sixteenth-century English forebears. Explanatory notes can help us to understand details as basic and mundane as first-century Palestinian burial customs (notes to Mark 16:1-5), or as difficult and elusive as the thought-patterns of men and women in ancient cultures worlds removed from our own.

New theories and discoveries about these thought-patterns can sometimes put explanatory notes at odds with traditional interpretations. Sometimes the notes themselves change with changing times. One telling example is worth a brief visit.

1 Corinthians 14:33b-36

In the continuing debate in Christian churches over the role of women in ministry, few New Testament passages stand out as much as Paul's admonition to "all the churches of the saints":

> (As in all the churches of the saints, women should be silent in the churches. For they are not permitted to speak, but should be subordinate, as the law also says. If there is anything they desire to know, let them ask their husbands at home. For it is shameful for a woman to speak in church. Or did the word of God originate with you? Or are you the only ones it has reached?)

As forthright as this passage seems, it is also puzzling. Paul's letters are full of praise for specific women who lead house congregations. In 1 Corinthians 11:5 and elsewhere, Paul reports that women were active in leading worship in Corinth. Why would he reverse himself here? The Oxford annotator John Reumann (revising the work of his predecessor, the late John Knox) acknowledges the issue in his notes:

> **14.33b-36** Since 11.5 reports that women had a role in worship at Corinth, some refer *women* here only to those married (see v. 35), or distinguish a house church in ch 11 from the total community in Corinth (v. 26), or take these culturally conditioned verses as an editorial insertion; see 1 Tim. 2.11-12. *(NOAB explanatory note)*

Reumann's note reflects a sea change in the attitudes taken toward controversial passages by the Oxford editors, one that reflects similar changes in the Episcopal Church and churches like it over the past three decades.

In his 1962 commentary, John Knox, then professor at the Union Theological Seminary in New York City, kept the annotation to a bare minimum:

34: 1 Tim. 2:11-12; 1 Pet. 3:1. **36:** Paul ends discussion of a troublesome issue in a similar way in 11:16 and Phil 3:15.

Recognizing that the role of women was a troublesome issue not only for the first-century Corinthians but for a growing number of present-day readers, Knox's note carefully avoids the fray. He says nothing about the contradictory passage at 11:5, and supplies without comment cross-references to two parallel passages that repeat the substance of these troublesome verses and also heighten the tone. The note remains unchanged in the 1973 edition.

Between 1962 and 1991, when the *New Oxford Annotated Bible* was published, tremendous changes occurred in many North American Protestant denominations regarding the place of women in ministry. For the first time in the history of any of the liturgical churches holding to the historic episcopate, the Episcopal Church admitted women to all ranks of the ordained clergy, having allowed women to vote and stand for office at General Convention only a few years earlier. At the same time, tumultuous changes were taking place in North American attitudes toward women in the workplace and in public life. No wonder that in this bracing atmosphere New Testament scholarship focused more and more on the cultures and world views that informed the ancient texts. Many in the church began to insist that biblical passages like this one be read as evidence of a particular cultural moment not immediately or easily translatable into the cultural conditions of our own.

The revised annotation on 1 Corinthians 14 closely reflects both the new knowledge of women's history and changed attitudes toward women in society that have developed over the past thirty years. The 1991 translation even puts verses 33a-36 in parentheses, lending implicit support to the possibility that the command to silence is an interpolation into Paul's text made by others. Many New Testament scholars believe the strictures have been imported from 1 Timothy 2:11-12, a letter ascribed to Paul but almost universally considered to have been written by one of his followers years after Paul's death. Verses 33a-36 appear at different places in different ancient manuscripts (see translator's note *h*), suggesting that the passage may have been free-floating from the start.

As usual, the Oxford annotation on this passage below the bar-line is terse and relatively noncommittal. It reports alternative solutions to the problem, and presents no direct solution of its own. But that the annotation mentions even the possibility of culturally conditioned verses or editorial insertions demonstrates how far behind we have left the world of James I, or for that matter, the strained objectivity of the 1962 note. The application of critical analysis and women's historical experiences in reading the Bible can radically modify the traditional view of a biblical text and call into question the way we regard the authority of the Bible itself.

New developments in reading the Bible can be exciting to many, but they can also be unsettling and alarming to others. Not all Bible readers are comfortable with these newly contextualized readings. Although lives are seldom at stake over the interpretation of verses of Scripture as they were in the sixteenth century (at least for "first-world" Anglicans), shifts in theological attitudes that are reflected in Bible commentaries still have political consequences. Here is a small but significant one. The 1962 edition of the Oxford Bible bore the descriptive motto "An Ecumenical Study Bible," reflecting Roman Catholic and Eastern Orthodox cooperation in its preparation and distribution. Their participation seems now to be at an end. The 1962 motto has been silently dropped from the 1991 title page.

Chapter Six

Reading the Bible,
Reading Scripture

O Lord, perfect your work in me. Open to me the pages
of your book. (St. Augustine, *Confessions*, 11.2)

In reading the Bible, as in everything else, learning to use
the tools of the trade is not the same as doing the work.
The typefaces and layouts and graphics and annotations of
our contemporary Bibles provide essential equipment for
the act of reading, but they cannot substitute for it. This
brings us to the larger issue of this book. What is it that
we are doing when we say we are reading Scripture? What
do we mean when at a Sunday eucharist we respond
"Thanks be to God" to a reading from the Old or New
Testament as "the Word of the Lord"?

To answer that question, put aside for a moment the
complex printed page of your annotated Bible, and meditate again on the act of reading itself.

∼ Reading Silently, Reading Aloud
Imagine a reader reading. It doesn't matter where. Readers
are everywhere. Not only in places we would expect—the
inner sanctum of a monastic library, say, or deep in the

shadows of an old-fashioned curtained bed—but also in the most public of spaces. A boy squats on a pile of discarded newspapers cast haphazardly on a garbage heap, absorbed in a comic book. A man folds his overcoat into a seat cushion, and sits reading on the steps of a crowded plaza, oblivious to the traffic noise around him. A woman reads intently while walking down the street, skillfully negotiating thick pedestrian traffic.

Watching someone read, one is often struck by what seems an unassailable self-sufficiency, a stillness, a kind of entrancement.[1] To interrupt a reader would be like breaking a spell. Self-possessed themselves, readers also possess the objects they read. They hold their purchase or their gift or their discovery in their hands. They control what page they will read, and when. They are free to keep the book or to cast it aside. They are free to pay attention as they choose.

But anyone who reads knows too that books can possess their readers. How do books wield such power? What holds people rapt? Do they read because they have to, or do they read for pleasure? What are they reading? Whose voice do they hear? One cannot usually tell from watching, and the unspoken protocols of reading forbid our asking. What people read is an intimate matter.

Silence enforces that intimacy. Keeping silence is one of the first things we learn to do as we begin to read. For the most part, silence in our culture is rare, as rare as serious readers have become. Readers thirst for silence. Libraries and reading rooms are like churches, sanctuaries of voluntary silence, refuges for private readers, places impatient of restless chatter. But the silence of libraries and churches is not the only silence readers learn to keep. The act of reading itself is usually indistinguishable from silence. Many of us remember the burden placed on us as first graders not to follow the line of type with our fingers as we read, and more importantly, not to move our lips. Good reading means silent reading, and silent reading often means rapid reading. Few lovers of books could imagine reading otherwise, except on public occasions designated, oddly enough, as "readings"—a paper read aloud at a conference, a poetry reading, a Bible lesson read aloud in a church or synagogue. These public moments are exceptions that prove the rule. For the most part, reading is private, single, and silent.

But it was not always so. In a book profoundly shaped by the experience of reading the Bible, the fourth-century bishop and rhetorician Augustine of Hippo recalls his shock when he happened upon his mentor Ambrose, the Archbishop of Milan, reading silently in a book:

> When he read, his eyes scanned the page and his heart explored the meaning, but his voice was silent and his tongue was still. All could approach him freely and it was not usual for visitors to be announced, so that often, when we came to see him, we found him reading like this in silence, for he never read aloud.[2]

Augustine and his fellow competitors for the great man's time would stare in quiet amazement, waiting for the spell to break. It rarely did. "After a time we went away again, guessing that in the short time when he was free from the turmoil of other men's affairs and was able to refresh his own mind, he would not wish to be distracted."

Ambrose's silence is inscrutable to Augustine. Was Ambrose reading some obscure or difficult passage, and keeping silence so that he would not be bothered to answer the questions of less learned inquirers? After all, an archbishop's private time was precious. Or did he read silently to spare his voice, "which quite easily became hoarse"?

Ambrose's cultural standing and political clout as Arch-bishop of Milan made him the equal of any secular official in the region. A trained, commanding voice was an essential instrument of power for a cosmopolitan fourth-century archbishop. What Ambrose read and how he read mattered deeply to an ambitious man like Augustine. His sense of wonder "belongs...to a man who believed that the way to the truth was through the written word as performed or interpreted within a community."[3] Completely in keeping with his own provincial training as a rhetorician, Augustine assumes that anyone who reads reads aloud, and reads for an audience. For someone of Augustine's training and background, Ambrose's silent reading was a mystery.

Most fourth-century readers of the *Confessions* would have shared Augustine's puzzlement, and so would their biblical ancestors. In the several centuries when the texts that comprise the Hebrew Bible and the documents of the New Testament were being collected in their final form, from the fourth century BCE right through and beyond the time of Augustine, the experience of reading would have been for most people an experience not of silence, but of sound. Every text demanded not just a reader but a speaker and a hearer, even if that hearer were the reader speaking to herself (for there were women readers as well as men), listening in privacy to the sound of her own voice. More often, there would be a group of listeners, gathered ex-pressly to hear the words of the chronicler or the law-giver or the prophet or the poet or the storyteller. Even though these cultures prized the writings of poets, philosophers, historians, and prophets, lovingly preserving their texts on scrolls and in codices, they nonetheless regarded the act of reading itself primarily as an oral experience. The reading of a text created a community, just as surely as the needs of different communities helped to shape various kinds of texts. As an oral and aural experience, reading was by its very nature a shared enterprise—a social, religious, and oftentimes political affair.

The biblical writings themselves present substantial evidence of reading as an oral activity both private and public: the very word for reading in Hebrew implies both an act of hearing and an act of speech.[4] The portrayal of an act of reading as a scene of hearing and speaking as well as of seeing is so commonplace in the Bible as to seem unremarkable.

But most such moments in the Bible are intentionally public, occurring at strategic moments when the community seems ripe for reformation and renewal. In the second book of Kings, with all Jerusalem gathered around him, the young reformer King Josiah reads aloud the "book of the covenant," newly discovered in the course of repairs the king had ordered to the Temple fabric (2 Kings 23). In a later, even more dramatic incident, recorded in the book of Jeremiah, King Jehoiakim is furious that Jeremiah's predictions of destruction had been read from a scroll "in the hearing of the people" by Jeremiah's secretary Baruch. The king orders the scroll seized, and has it read aloud to him in his private chamber. As soon as his assistant had read three or four columns, "the king would cut them off with a penknife and throw them into the fire in the brazier, until the entire scroll was consumed" (Jeremiah 36:23). Fiercely demonstrating the indestructibility of God's word, Jeremiah retaliates by dictating the entire scroll again, and then adding to it.[5]

As Josiah proclaims a renewed Torah from the ancient scroll in the Temple, or as Jeremiah writes and rewrites words that speak truth to power, we witness the Hebrew Bible coming into being. A climactic moment in the process can be found in the book of Nehemiah, which together with the book of Ezra tells of the struggles to rebuild the Jewish community in the land of Israel after the return of the Jewish exiles from Babylon. In the midst of the rebuilding, the narrator recounts how Ezra the priest brought "the book of the law of Moses" before a huge assembly of men and women at the Water Gate in Jerusalem, and read it in its entirety from early morning until midday. As the great city was rebuilt to celebrate the end of exile, so too the great book of the law of God was compiled in close to its final form. Since by this time Aramaic, not Hebrew, had become the everyday language of the people, the text of the law required translation and interpretation: "So they read from the book, from the law of God, with interpretation. They gave the sense, so that the people understood the reading" (Nehemiah 8:8).

These striking episodes give compelling evidence of the oral, public quality of reading in biblical times, but they also mark the increasing importance of the sacred writing itself as both the occasion and the script for public affirmations of faith. We hear and watch as script becomes Scripture, the "book of the law of Moses" becomes the Torah, a writing that will unleash its power to reform and renew Israel every time it is voiced aloud in the presence of the believing congregation.

In the New Testament, there is a scene of reading more intimate than any of these, one that reveals much about the path that Christian Bible reading would take. In Luke's book of Acts the apostle Philip, led by the Spirit, overhears a wealthy Ethiopian eunuch reading aloud in the solitude of his own chariot from his personal copy of an Isaiah scroll. The eunuch is a high court official, we are told, from a faraway country. He is both charismatic and exotic—a man who spends his life close to power but in the middle of Palestine seems strangely out of place. His extraordinary "otherness" is part of the point of the story: a leading motif in Luke is the sharing of the gospel with the "nations," those who were not part of the historic people of Israel. As he stands in his chariot, reading from a Greek scroll, the Ethiopian eunuch emerges as a potent image of many contemporary Bible readers—new to the Bible, sophisticated, curious, eager to learn, but very much on the outside, looking in on what seems to be an insider's book. It is no accident that Luke should place the encounter between Philip and the eunuch on a "wilderness road" at the threshold of the desert, always a proper site for the testing of the self. Both the Ethiopian trying to read and Philip, the apostle adept in reading, are portrayed as fellow pilgrims on the way, or *hodos*, the Greek word that echoes throughout this passage. In early Christian writing, *hodos* signifies not only a physical road but also a spiritual way—the Christians were people who were following the Way, or, as the Hebrew Bible so often puts it, they were people seeking to "walk in the way of the Lord." For Christian believers, that Way was now made clear in the death and resurrection of Jesus.

This moment of private reading on a wilderness road turns out to be a moment of life-changing decision. As in Luke's story of Jesus reading in the synagogue (Luke 4), this stranger reads aloud a prophetic passage from the book of Isaiah, a passage that seems to say more than what it says:

> So Philip ran up to [his chariot] and heard him reading the prophet Isaiah. He asked, "Do you understand what you are reading?" He replied, "How can I, unless someone guides me?" And he invited Philip to get in and sit beside him. (Acts 8:30-31)

The scene of private reading becomes a scene of holy conversation. Philip doesn't merely see the Ethiopian reading; he hears him. Just as the act of reading in antiquity was both private and public, so too the act of understanding demands conversation—a conversation that Luke presents as a kind of conversion. Puzzling over Isaiah's description of the sheep led to the slaughter, and the lamb silent before its shearer, the Ethiopian eunuch, a stranger to the sacred page, seems almost by intuition to understand that the text means more than it seems to mean.

> Now the passage of the scripture that he was reading was this:
> "Like a sheep he was led to the slaughter,
>   and like a lamb silent before its shearer,
>   so he does not open his mouth.
> In his humiliation justice was denied him.
>   Who can describe his generation?
>   For his life is taken away from the earth."
> The eunuch asked Philip, "About whom, may I ask you, does the prophet say this, about himself or about someone else?" Then Philip began to speak, and starting with this scripture, he proclaimed to him the good news about Jesus. As they were going along the road, they came to some water; and the eunuch said, "Look, here is water! What is to prevent me from being baptized?" (Acts 8:32-37)

It seems an odd place for the episode to go. What does reading Scripture have to do with being baptized? One is reminded here of the incident recounted earlier in Luke, when a mysterious stranger unfolds the full meaning of Scripture to the pilgrims on the road to Emmaus—a meaning they only fully understand when it is given flesh and sinew in the breaking of the bread. Here too, in this episode in Acts, a scene of reading culminates in what we now have come to call a "sacramental" action: an outward sign of God's inward grace received through the water of baptism. In Luke's gospel, reading the Bible is never a passive action. Nor is reading it an end in itself. The act of reading is a beginning, not an end. It opens an entrance into a sacred conversation, and leads to the conversion of a life now spent "on the Way."[6]

～ The Voices of the Page

To learn to read the Bible in community is to learn to open ourselves to this ancient connection between conversation and conversion. We must try to recover what might be called a biblical experience of active reading.

For this kind of reading there is ample precedent. In ancient times, it was impossible to read without the sense that you were being engaged by a living voice. Even the act of writing was an oral and aural affair. Few "writers" in antiquity actually put pen to paper. A writer as rhetorically sophisticated as Paul of Tarsus dictated his words to a scribe or *amanuensis*, and this had been common practice for centuries. Baruch, Jeremiah's *sofer*, or secretary, not only took down Jeremiah's words, but became himself a participant in Jeremiah's story. Five hundred years later, when the apostle Paul writes a postscript to his letter to the Galatian congregation ("See what large letters I make when I am writing in my own hand!"), the action constitutes a dramatic and unusual departure, stressing the urgency of the case he was pressing against his opponents.

Even as they took shape in their final canonical form in the second and third centuries CE, both the Hebrew Bible and the New Testament writings were meant to be heard as they were read. We have already seen the influence of oral recitation of the Torah in the development of *ketib* and *qere.* From biblical times until well into the Middle Ages in Europe, most acts of reading would resemble the performing or hearing of a script than the rapid, silent reading of a printed text that has become the norm in modern times.

The oral bias of early Judaism and early Christianity is discernible even from the look of the surviving documents. We have already noted that Hebrew writing is consonantal. Anyone reading from the Torah in the synagogue would need to know the vowels by heart to pronounce the words correctly. Moreover, when they were writing in Greek, scribes and copyists usually wrote in continuous script, leaving no blank spaces between words or sentences. A reader would not think it unusual to encounter a sentence that was the Greek equivalent of the following:

INTHEBEGINNINGWASTHEWORD

This habit of continuous writing reveals the oral sensibility that a reader would bring to a manuscript of Scripture. One has to know what the text "says" in order to read the text properly, and the surest way to read the text properly is to read the text aloud. Try it. In the beginning was the Word, the Word spoken and heard long before it was read as we understand reading, even after it was committed to the page.

This oral sensibility remained vibrant throughout the Middle Ages and well into Reformation times. Although silent reading became a common practice in the writing rooms (*scriptoria*) of the monasteries to facilitate the efficient copying of manuscripts, it never displaced habits of oral reading, particularly in settings of worship and meditation. Many twelfth- and thirteenth-century illuminated manuscripts show people reading in groups. As one historian writes, "To read in groups was to read aloud; to read alone was to mumble."[7] Whether reading communally in chapel or privately in a monastic cell, the monk attended to what were called the "voices of the page." In medieval Latin usage, the word "to read," *legere*, seems interchangeable with the word "to hear," *audire*. When used without other explanation in medieval texts, words like *legere* and *lectio* mean "an activity which, like chant and writing, requires the participation of the whole body and the whole mind":

> For the ancients, to meditate is to read a text and to learn it "by heart" in the fullest sense of this expression, that is, with one's own being: with the body, since the mouth pronounced it, with the memory which fixes it, with the intelligence which understands its meaning, and with the will which desires to put it into practice.[8]

In monastic practice, this kind of reading came to be known as *lectio divina*, divine or holy reading. When the English monk Bede used the ancient metaphor of chewing or rumination to describe the reading of the sacred text, he had *lectio divina* as his model. It is a kind of reading that permits the text to inhabit the reader's being. As Jean Leclercq describes it, such reading demands a memorizing of the sacred text that depends not just on visual memory but on muscular and aural memory as well. Reading in the monastic mode, even reading in private, was an active process: "It is what inscribes, so to speak, the sacred text in the body and in the soul."[9] It is analogous to the traditional Jewish practice called *davening*, when the worshiper who is reading or chanting the biblical text sways his body gently as he reads; or the profound bow the Muslim makes as he intones the words of the holy Qu'ran. This active reading was the rule rather than the exception in the Middle Ages, and is in continuity with practices in biblical times.

Even Reformation thinkers who rejected the monastic institutions that made such active reading possible still understood the process of reading Scripture in aural rather than visual terms. For Martin Luther, the voices of the page still spoke clearly and with power. Trained as an Augustinian monk, Luther preached to the end the monastic ideal of active reading. For Luther, to read the Bible or to translate it was to pray the Bible, and to pray the Bible was to memorize it, to know it with heart and soul and mind and mouth and ear. When meditating, he wrote, "always repeat the oral speech and the literal word in the Book and compare them with each other, not only in your heart, but outwardly, read them and reread them with diligent attentiveness and reflection [to see] what the Holy Spirit means by them."[10]

Closely related to ancient and medieval forms of meditation and *ruminatio*, Luther's practice of active reading was firmly grounded in what can be called a scriptural theology. But his lively sense of reading the Bible as an active, oral experience proved difficult to sustain in a time when communities of readers began to fragment and multiply. Even before the advent of printing, the reading public had begun to change. The release from the sometimes harsh disciplines of monastic reading, coupled with the questioning of the institutional interpretations imposed by a universal church with a single point of view, unleashed extraordinary new intellectual and artistic energies.

～ Open Books, Closed Minds

After the Reformation, habits of Bible reading moved in two opposite directions. Following the intellectual breakthroughs of the eighteenth-century European Enlightenment, there was an explosion of knowledge about the Bible: the sources of biblical writings, the history of interpretation, archaeology, oral traditions, and the way written documents could transform those traditions. Earlier in this book, as we negotiated the annotated Bible page, we experienced at first hand the benefits of this knowledge explosion. But as knowledge about the Bible increased, many scholars began to treat texts once thought sacred and inviolable just as rigorously (and sometimes just as skeptically) as they would any other kind of historical or literary document. They developed complex and exciting ways of separating authentic historical material from the myths and theological interpretations in which it was couched in the ancient writings. In the late nineteenth century especially, this activity centered around what was known as the "quest for the historical Jesus," a quest, as we have seen, that has powerfully reemerged in biblical scholarship over the last several years, provoking the same kinds of controversy now as it did a hundred years ago. With the increasing secularity of the academic institutions that sponsor such studies, it was more and more difficult to connect the results of historical criticism with the spiritual lives of believers, even when those believers were the biblical critics themselves.

Developing at the same time, and in some ways as a reaction to this kind of thinking, was a new literalism in reading the Bible, with roots deep in the radical Reformation. The slogan *sola scriptura*, "by Scripture alone," became a battle-cry for those who rejected almost entirely the role of tradition in interpreting the biblical text.[11] With the ascendancy of biblical criticism in the universities and seminaries, literalists who once expressed antipathy toward "tradition" (that is, the sort of allegorical readings that were identified with the medieval *Glossa)*, now transferred their mistrust to the sometimes radically revisionist views made possible by new scholarship. This literalist sensibility is as old as the biblical writings themselves, and has sometimes proved itself a valuable balance to the relentless unravelling and dissection of beloved texts. But strong literalist convictions also led many readers, especially in America, to disavow critical analysis altogether. Literalist readers share a deep and often unexamined faith in the transparency of biblical writing; they hold that nothing blocks the reader from seeing through the words on the page directly to their intended meaning. This insistence on the "perspicuity" and inerrancy of the Bible can be just as alienating and misleading as the academic biblical critic's discomfort with traditional religious commitment.

It is easy to caricature either movement, and I do not mean to do so here. Each has had a powerful effect on the way Anglicans view the Bible. This is also true for most Protestant denominations in the United States, where both the literalist and the analytical points of view dovetail with the deep individualism of American life. It is an individualism indebted to the fierce independence of mind that created Tyndale's first translation in the 1520s, and was transmitted to the American colonies by the generations of Protestant dissenters who first emigrated to these shores, clutching their Geneva Bibles. The theologian Stanley Hauerwas argues that biblical literalism and biblical criticism have much in common as ideologies "in the service of the fictive agent of the Enlightenment—namely, the rational individual—who believes that truth in general (and particularly the truth of the Christian faith) can be known without initiation into a community that requires transformation of the self."[12]

Both biblical literalism and biblical criticism, although diametrically opposite in their rhetorical stances, share common roots in the rationalist traditions that have shaped western churches since the Reformation. And they have had remarkably similar effects on the history of Bible reading, many of them negative. "Open books, in some instances, led to closed minds": this acerbic insight from a distinguished historian of the printed book pinpoints the irony of Gutenberg's great achievement.[13] In the age of the printed book, privately owned and silently read, Bible reading is transformed into a private activity. Liberals and conservatives draw up battlelines across the contested territory of the sacred page. Readers of the Bible either feel compelled to take sides or decide against entering the fray at all. Many thoughtful people, including many Episcopalians, feel torn between literalist and analytical ways of reading the Bible. The loss of the social dimension of reading, particularly in the Protestant churches, has made the Bible itself seem unapproachable, all but unreadable.

Is it possible to make the Bible readable again? Earlier I implied that for centuries the act of reading the Bible demanded the same kind of energies as performance from a script. The comparison was not meant to be disrespectful or flip. *Scriptio*, script, scripture—all are linked. Religious communities that treasure the written word also treasure its recitation. There is always a dynamic relationship between the written word of Scripture and its oral performance, a relationship embedded in the life of a religious community:

> No text, written, oral, or both, is sacred or authoritative in isolation from a community. A text is only "scripture" insofar as a group of persons perceives it to be sacred or holy, powerful and meaningful.... What is scripture for one group may be a meaningless, nonsensical, or even perversely false text for another.[14]

In view of this definition, it is useful to make a distinction between reading the Bible and reading the Bible as

Scripture. The activities are complementary but distinct. As with any text considered sacred, whether the Qu'ran or the Puranas or the Book of Mormon, to read the Bible and to read it accurately, one first has to understand what is on the printed page and how it came to be there. That is the kind of thing that we began earlier in this book, learning to use the tools available on a typical annotated Bible page. Reading the Bible is demanding. You can explore the history of its texts and how they have been edited. You can critically evaluate the nuances of the various English translations. You can get a feel for the characteristic rhetorical and interpretive strategies of the biblical writers. You can try to understand how they themselves read and responded to the biblical literature that they inherited. You can acknowledge that faithful readers can sometimes come to opposite conclusions about how a text is to be interpreted, and that all interpretations have histories. All this provides crucial groundwork for anyone who wants to read the Bible with accuracy and integrity, and it can be very exciting. It is work that can continue through a lifetime of reading, and the kind of work that every Bible reader needs to do.

But reading the Bible this way is not the same as reading Scripture.

∿ Reading the Script, Hearing the Play

Let me offer an analogy from the theater. Shakespeare's *Hamlet* was first produced about the time that James I came to the throne, and was probably performed before the king at Hampton Court in 1604, by a lovely coincidence the same year that James commissioned his new translation of the Bible. Like the committee of translators the king would soon appoint, Shakespeare's acting company, the King's Men, was under James's direct patronage and protection.

If you open to a page in any modern annotated edition of *Hamlet*, you will be struck by its physical similarity to the Bible pages we have been discussing. The edition I use, which is the one-volume Signet edition of the complete plays, lays out the page in columns, just like an annotated Bible. The acts, scenes, and lines are carefully numbered, in the manner of biblical chapters and verses. There are careful textual notes gathered in a headnote to the play (the textual history of *Hamlet* seems almost as complicated as that of Mark!), along with careful explanatory notes at the bottom of each column. Like biblical commentaries, these notes explicate difficult or obsolete words, point to particularly vexed textual problems, refer the reader to other scenes in Shakespeare's plays for contrast and comparison, and refrain as much as possible from interpretive comment, assuming that such comment is the task of the reader.

From the appearance of the page, therefore, *Hamlet* seems to be complete in itself, stable, fixed, and unchanging. But in fact, the truth is more complex. As elegant and finished as the printed page appears, what you read on the page is only part of the story. The Signet edition of *Hamlet* was not the *Hamlet* that Shakespeare wrote. Like the text of Mark 16, the text of Shakespeare's play on the page before you is the product of generations of scholars making difficult choices among rival versions. Although no manuscript of Shakespeare's survives, four printed editions do. They appeared between 1603, about the time the play was first produced on the stage of the Globe Theater, and 1623, seven years after Shakespeare's death, when the first collected edition of his plays was published.

That there are any printed editions at all is itself a breakthrough. It was one thing to prepare the Geneva Bible for publication in 1576, editing the commentary, setting the type, proofreading the text, registering the publication with the required government agency, printing the book, and selling it. It was quite another thing to publish something so ephemeral (and often so politically subversive) as a play, much less to publish it in anything like the Signet layout, which rivals in complexity that of the Bible itself. For a late twentieth-century reader, such complexity lends the edition (and its author) a certain prestige.

In Shakespeare's time plays were popular, but they were not prestigious. Besides, the untimely publication of a popular play might have meant fiscal disaster. Plays like *Hamlet* were valuable property for the theatrical companies that commissioned, produced, and performed them. Aside from the political hassles of publishing in the London of Elizabeth and James (especially publishing a play, given Puritan opposition to the decadence of going to plays), competitive stage companies like the King's Men, in which Shakespeare was a principal stockholder, held onto these scripts as primary assets. When the play was in production, there was probably only a single manuscript copy, in the form of a prompt book, jealously guarded by the company. To print it while the play was still in production could result in financial suicide, as rival companies could snatch it up and produce it on their own; no copyright laws protected the author's profits. In fact, one pirated copy of the play did get into circulation, perhaps reconstructed from memory by a member of another company who recorded the lines he recalled immediately upon leaving a performance. That publication would have created considerable consternation among the King's Men, who perhaps saw to it that another edition was published a year later, "newly imprinted and enlarged to almost as much again as it was, according to the true and perfect copy."

What was the "true and perfect copy"? Perhaps it was the prompt book, commandeered from its secure place attached to the wall of the "tiring room," as the backstage dressing room at the Globe was called. Perhaps it was an actual manuscript of Shakespeare's, part of what the Elizabethans called "foul papers" or rough drafts, from which an author would then make a "true and perfect" final version. More likely, it was a combination of all these things, plus changes made in the heat of performance, or second thoughts of the playwright himself. We will never know. This second edition was reprinted in 1611. But the edition of 1623 shows significant differences from all of these, and perhaps uses a new transcript prepared independently of the previous printed editions, using the foul papers and the prompt book.[15]

Why was this printing history so convoluted? Because, in spite of all the energy publication demanded, the printed script was in fact secondary to the performance of the play itself—and the play was a matter to be heard, not read. And what was heard was the result not of a single author's pen but of a complex act of collaboration, including the playwright with his written script, the producers with their financial demands, the actors with their interpretive skills, and the audience with its skills in listening, watching, and responding. Reading a play was never a solitary or private matter. For all the sometimes elaborate and expensive visual spectacle available to a seventeenth-century audience, it was always said that the audience gathered to "hear" a play rather than to "see" it, much less read it. Even in a culture bursting with the possibilities of print, where it was now possible to cultivate the art of reading as a private, solitary act, the oral and aural sensibilities that we have seen embodied in biblical writing itself did not disappear in Reformation England, particularly in the theater. If anything, they deepened.

To experience the full force of scenes like this in *Hamlet*, it is necessary to hear and see the play as well as to read it. That is the nature of a script. Even though all the scholarly apparatus allows the text of the play to be preserved on the printed page, the play *Hamlet* is not the play as written. It is the play as performed. The written text was from the first secondary to the living performance. An authentic performance depends on the effective collaboration of the playwright, producers, and actors in creating the action. But such performance also depends on the effective collaboration of the audience, who bring to the performance an understanding of theatrical language and convention without which such a performance would make little or no sense at all.

Can the double experience of reading *Hamlet* and hearing the play performed help us understand the experience of reading Scripture?

∼ Take It and Read

Despite all the energy lavished on them by their editors and the devotion shown by their audiences, Shakespeare's scripts are not sacred texts. But the multiple demands made upon those who would hear and see these scripts performed bear a striking resemblance to demands made upon those who would hear and understand the Bible as Christians participating fully in a community of Christian readers. Reading the Bible accurately is even more difficult and time-consuming an enterprise than reading a page of Shakespeare. The Bible consists of texts far more ancient than Shakespeare's, written in languages and for cultures that are worlds removed from our own. Simply to understand what the text says takes a considerable amount of staying power. For that kind of work it is crucial to take full advantage of all the scholarly apparatus we have been describing.

But learning to read your way through an annotated Bible is not the same as reading Scripture. It only prepares you for it. Reading Scripture is a religious act. Critical analysis and understanding precede it, but do not substitute for it. Neglecting or refusing to read critically and analytically makes the Bible a closed book. But reading critically and analytically just for its own sake can render Scripture mute.

As Anglicans, the most fruitful community of Scripture readers we can create must be at the same time detached from and engaged by what we read. As faithful readers of Scripture we must acknowledge the dark places, the inconsistencies, and the downright foreignness of our ancient texts. At the same time we must acknowledge our own inadequacies as readers; our indebtedness to tradition; our need to share what we know with others, and to own up to what we cannot know. And we must recognize and proclaim that the Spirit who inspired these texts, and continues to inspire its readers, is never predictable. The Spirit blows where the Spirit wills.

Think back to Augustine, standing in a corridor of Ambrose's archepiscopal palace, marveling that his mentor and protector could have the temerity to read silently and alone. That moment of awed surprise was a first step in Augustine's introduction to reading Scripture. Augustine knew about the Spirit: according to his own account, an act of reading converted him to Christianity. His life in crisis, he had retreated with his friend Alypius to the solitude of an enclosed garden. Augustine's careful description of the place recalls an earlier scene in the book: the youthful escapade where he and his friends had once invaded a neighbor's garden to steal some pears, a moment of transgression that becomes for him a symbol of his fallen state. Expert reader of Genesis that he is, it is no accident that he should set his experience of turning to God in the silence of a garden, and should find himself weeping in the shade of a fig tree. Sitting in solitude, he hears the distant, sing-song voice of a child playing a game: "Take it and read, take it and read." The voice stops him short. He rushes back to where he had left Alypius, and takes up the manuscript codex of Paul's epistles that he had abandoned there:

> I seized it and opened it, and in silence I read the first passage on which my eyes fell: *Not in reveling and drunkenness, not in lust and wantonness, not in quarrels and rivalries. Rather, arm yourselves with the Lord Jesus Christ; spend no more thought on nature and nature's appetites*. I had no wish to read more and no need to do so. For in an instant, as I came to the end of the sentence, it was as though the light of confidence flooded into my heart and all the darkness of doubt dispelled.[16]

Like Philip's encounter with the Ethiopian in Acts, this is a classic scene of reading as an act of conversion. It pays eloquent tribute to what Augustine learned from Ambrose about the wisdom (and power) of reading a passage in silence.

Although some of us may not have much sympathy for the moral scrupulosity that drove Augustine to abandon the mother of his child and seek conversion, his respect both for Scripture and for the limits of Scripture still speaks with tremendous power. To be open to hear the Word of God in Scripture as Augustine heard it demands both a clear head and an open mind. It requires spiritual formation and intellectual discipline. It also requires humility—a willingness to acknowledge what we do not know, and perhaps can never know. Such reading is the loving work of an informed heart. As a parishioner of mine once eloquently put it, no scriptural act of faith demands that you "check your brains at the door." To read Scripture faithfully, one must accept the full discipline of reading—with heart and mind and soul and mouth and ear, listening both for the voice of the Spirit who speaks through Scripture, and also for the voices of one's companions in faith, voices past and present, probing and respectful, agreeing and disagreeing both with you and with the sacred text before them.

So take courage. To be an active reader of Scripture, responding to the sacred page with heart and mind and soul and body, you do not need to be an adept rhetorician like Augustine, nor to enter a monastery. You do not need to undergo a dramatic conversion in a lonely garden, nor do you need to sacrifice the greatest gift that the inventors of printing gave to us—the ability to retreat to a quiet, private corner, book in hand, and enter a silent world of engrossed reflection. But you do need to enter the conversation. For a person of faith, even reading in solitude ushers you into a community of readers. It is like the voice of the *rebbe* summoning his students together in playful, earnest conversation around the Talmud page, or like the voice of a child on the other side of the garden wall calling for Augustine to take up the book and read. Reading Scripture means mastering a community's particular disciplines of reading, in order to join the life-giving conversation between God and God's creatures that the Bible records and its faithful readers continue.

The word "discipline" need not put you off. Mastering a discipline does not mean blindly submitting to authority or accepting other people's interpretations "on faith." To master the discipline of reading Scripture is more like mastering the discipline of playing Bach's cello suites, or acting the part of Hamlet, or perfecting the craft of cabinet-making, or learning to dance. Like all activities intrinsically worth doing, these demand energy, commitment, and a willingness to be taught. They can be solitary disciplines, demanding concentration, silence, full attention. To an observer, the musician, the cabinet-maker, or the dancer are as focused and self-absorbed as the most avid reader. But if these artists are solitary, they are never alone, any more than a solitary monk is ever alone reading Scripture quietly in his cell. They owe their mastery to generations of predecessors, equally disciplined, equally skilled. And they also owe their mastery to the living community of artists who share their gifts, to the mentors who help shape them, and to the even larger community of people who need and treasure them, critique them, and applaud them. The paradox of such discipline is that it grants the artist unparalleled freedom to pass beyond the skill of her mentors, even to alter the very shape of the discipline itself.

So too with readers of Scripture. Take up the Book and read. Strive to master the challenging disciplines of faithful reading. You may be solitary, but you are never isolated. And you are never really alone.

Endnotes

∼ Chapter 1

1. Article of Religion VI in *The Book of Common Prayer* (New York: Church Hymnal Corporation, 1979), 868. All further citations from the prayer book are from this edition unless otherwise noted, and will be cited in the text.

2. Quoted in William P. Haugaard, "The Bible in the Anglican Reformation," in Frederick Houk Borsch, ed., *Anglicanism and the Bible* (Wilton, Conn.: Morehouse Barlow, 1984), 14.

3. *Ibid.*, 76.

∼ Chapter 2

1. In keeping with interfaith practice, this book uses the phrase "Common Era" (CE) to refer to the centuries following Jesus' birth, and "Before the Common Era" (BCE) for the centuries preceding it.

2. Quoted in Stephen Greenblatt, "The Word of God in the Age of Mechanical Reproduction" in *Renaissance Self-Fashioning: From More to Shakespeare* (Chicago: University of Chicago Press, 1980), 96.

3. *Ibid.*, 74-114. For Greenblatt on "aura," see 85-86. The concept was first described by the great mid-twentieth-century critic Walter Benjamin.

4. *The New Oxford Annotated Bible, with the Apocrypha*, Bruce M. Metzger and Roland E. Murphy, eds. (New York: Oxford University Press, 1991). All Bible quotations are from this edition, unless otherwise noted. It is now available as a hypertext edition on CD-ROM, a new technology of the book that may change our ways of reading Scripture as dramatically as the manuscript codex or the printed *enchiridion* once did.

∾ Chapter 3

1.Gerald L. Bruns, *Invention, Writing, Textuality: Understanding in Literary History* (New Haven: Yale University Press, 1982), 29.

2. See Daniel Boyarin, *A Radical Jew: Paul and the Politics of Identity* (Berkeley: University of California Press, 1994), 100.

3.This discussion has been shaped by the opening chapters of Gabriel Josipovici's *The Book of God: A Response to the Bible* (New Haven and London: Yale University Press, 1988).

∾ Chapter 4

1. See Bruce Metzger's comment "To the Reader" in the *New Oxford Annotated Bible*, xii.

2. I am grateful to Professor Richard Corney of the General Theological Seminary in New York City for this suggestion.

3. Victor Roland Gold, *et al*, eds., *The New Testament and Psalms: An Inclusive Version* (New York: Oxford University Press, 1995), xvi. The editors discuss their principles in full in their General Introduction, vii–xxii.

4. Frank Kermode, *The Genesis of Secrecy: On the Interpretation of Narrative* (Cambridge: Harvard University Press, 1979), 66.

5. *Ibid.*, 72. The phrase "the sense of an ending" comes from his earlier book, *The Sense of an Ending: Studies in the Theory of Fiction* (Oxford: Oxford University Press, 1967/1975).

~ Chapter 5

1. Jonathan Boyarin, "Voices around the Text: The Ethnography of Reading at Mesivta Tigereth Jerusalem," in Jonathan Boyarin, ed., *The Ethnography of Reading* (Berkeley: University of California Press, 1993), 230.

2. Beryl Smalley, *The Study of the Bible in the Middle Ages* (Oxford: Basil Blackwell, 1952), 66. Smalley reproduces a page from a manuscript *Glossa* on St. John's Gospel produced in England in the late twelfth century, facing page 56.

3. Dante, "Letter to Can Grande della Scala," in Allen H. Gilbert, ed., *Literary Criticism: Plato to Dryden* (Detroit: Wayne State University Press, 1962), 202-203.

4. Dante, *The Divine Comedy: Purgatorio*, Charles S. Singleton, ed. and trans. (Princeton: Princeton University Press, 1973), 2:48/14-15.

5. Quoted in Evelyn B. Tribble, *Margins and Marginality: The Printed Page in Early Modern England* (Charlottesville: The University Press of Virginia, 1993), 14. For the discussion of Tyndale I have drawn on pages 14-17 of Tribble's book.

6. *Ibid.,* 17.

7. Quoted in Greenblatt, "The Word of God," 106.

8. "A Fruitfull Exhortation to the Reading and Knowledge of Holy Scripture," in Ronald B. Bond, ed., *Certain Sermons or Homilies (1547): A Critical Edition* (Toronto: University of Toronto Press, 1987), 62.

~ Chapter 6

1. For a helpful, rather playful description of the "reading trance," see the recent study by Victor Nell, *Lost in a Book: The Psychology of Reading for Pleasure* (New Haven: Yale University Press, 1988), 1-4.

2. All quotations from Augustine's *Confessions* are from the translation by R. S. Pine-Coffin (Harmondsworth, Middlesex: Penguin, 1974).

3. Nicholas Howe, "The Cultural Construction of Reading in Anglo-Saxon England," in J. Boyarin, *Ethnography of Reading*, 61. Howe offers an excellent discussion of this famous passage; every discussion of reading in antiquity that I have seen gives an account of this striking episode. Besides Howe's, the most helpful have been Bernard M. W. Knox, "Silent Reading in Antiquity," *Greek, Roman and Byzantine Studies* 9 (1968), 421-435; and Paul Saenger, "Silent Reading: Its Impact on Late Medieval Script and Society," *Viator* 13 (1982), 367-414.

4. Daniel Boyarin, "Placing Reading: Ancient Israel and Medieval Europe," in J. Boyarin, *Ethnography of Reading*, 11.

5. The Oxford annotators think that what Jeremiah wrote and what the king heard is probably preserved, along with other material, in our present chapters 1-25.

6. My reading of this passage in Acts relies on the following studies: Joseph B. Tyson, "Jews and Judaism in Luke-Acts: Reading as a Godfearer," *New Testament Studies* 41 (1995), 19-38; Frank M. Snowden, *Before Color Prejudice: The Ancient View of Blacks* (Cambridge: Cambridge University Press, 1983). I borrow the phrase "scene of reading" from Susan Noakes, "Gracious Words: Luke's Jesus and the Reading of Sacred Poetry at the Beginning of the Christian Era," in J. Boyarin, *Ethnography of Reading*, 38-57.

7. Saenger, "Silent Reading," 379-380.

8. Jean Leclercq, OSB, *The Love of Learning and the Desire for God*, trans. Catharine Misrahi (New York: Fordham University Press, 1961), 21-22.

9. *Ibid.*, 90.

10. Quoted in William A. Graham, *Beyond the Written Word: Oral Aspects of Scripture in the History of Religion* (Cambridge: Cambridge University Press, 1987), 149. My arguments about the nature of Scripture in this chapter are deeply indebted to Graham's work in this field.

11. Alister McGrath, *Reformation Thought: An Introduction* (Oxford: Basil Blackwell, 1988), 106.

12. Stanley Hauerwas, *Unleashing the Scriptures: Freeing the Bible from Captivity in America* (Nashville: Abingdon Press, 1993), 35.

13. Elizabeth L. Eisenstadt, *The Printing Press as an Agent of Change: Communications and Cultural Transformations in Early Modern Europe* (Cambridge: Cambridge University Press, 1979), 1:366.

14. William A. Graham, "Scripture," in Mircea Eliade, ed., *The Encyclopedia of Religion* (New York: Macmillan, 1987), 13:134.

15. I rely here on the exhaustive treatment of these matters in Stanley Wells, Gary Taylor, *et al.*, eds., *William Shakespeare: A Textual Companion* (Oxford: Clarendon Press, 1987), 396–420.

16. Augustine, *Confessions* 8.12.

Resources

There are many books to guide your initial forays into the world of the Bible. Here are a few that reflect some of the themes of *Opening the Bible*.

∼ Introductory Works

The best compass and road map to biblical materials for the beginner can be found in Etienne Charpentier, *How to Read the Old Testament* (Crossroads, 1987) and *How to Read the New Testament* (Crossroads, 1986). A short (and inexpensive) "reading plan" is also provided by David E. Johnson in *Opening the Hebrew Scriptures* and *Opening the New Testament* (Forward Movement, 1990), who aims his books at what he calls "the recovery of biblical literacy" for Episcopalians. In *The Bible* (Cambridge University Press, 1991), Stephen Prickett and Robert Barnes offer a concise and well-written guide to reading the Bible book by book. The third volume in this teaching series, Michael Johnston's *Engaging the Word* (Cowley,1997), will help you get started on group Bible study and offers keys to unlocking biblical texts.

For biblical criticism, especially the historical method, again the best introduction for the beginner is Charpentier, *How To Read the Old Testament*. See also E. P. Sanders and

Margaret Davies, *Studying the Synoptic Gospels* (Trinity Press International, 1989). The essential tool for this work remains Burton L. Throckmorton, *Gospel Parallels: A Comparison of the Synoptic Gospels*, 5th ed. (Nelson, 1992); this most recent edition uses the NRSV as its text. Most good libraries will provide access not only to *The Anchor Bible Dictionary* and *The Oxford Companion to the Bible*, but also to *The New Interpreter's Commentary*; *The New Jerome Biblical Commentary*; *The Interpreter's Dictionary of the Bible*; and the *Cambridge Companion to the Bible* (Cambridge University Press, 1997). Reflecting the best of contemporary biblical scholarship, these works are well-written, well-organized, and immediately useful to the non-specialist.

A very different kind of book, written from a Jewish perspective, also develops many topics I have touched on here: Burton L. Visotsky's *Reading the Book: Making the Bible a Timeless Text* (Anchor Books, 1991). Rabbi Visotsky collaborated with journalist Bill Moyers in producing the series on Genesis for public television. Peter Gomes, chaplain of Harvard University, has written a provocative and intelligent book that reflects the best of progressive Protestant thinking on the Bible: *The Good Book* (William Morrow, 1996).

For literary and imaginative approaches to the Hebrew scriptures, see the books of Robert Alter: *The Art of Biblical Narrative* (Basic Books, 1981); *The Art of Biblical Poetry* (Basic Books, 1985); and *The World of Biblical Literature* (Basic Books, 1992). Alter is a master in conveying the power and nuance of the original Hebrew. For an unusually powerful attempt to describe the God of the Hebrew Bible from a literary point of view, see Jack Miles, *God: A Biography* (Knopf, 1995). The late Canadian literary critic Northrop Frye presents an overwhelmingly Christianizing view of the Old Testament in *The Great Code: The Bible and*

Literature (Harcourt, Brace Jovanovich, 1982). A discussion that is more sensitive to Jewish traditions of reading Hebrew scriptures can be found in Gabriel Josipovici's *The Book of God: A Response to the Bible* (Yale University Press, 1988).

∼ The Lectionary and Daily Office

Many Episcopalians try to make a habit of reciting Morning and Evening Prayer as a way of organizing their Bible reading, using the lectionary as described in *The Book of Common Prayer* on pages 934-935. To read the Bible in this way is also to pray the Bible, making its diction, images, and themes a part of your daily life with God. The daily recitation of three or four psalms will allow these ancient hymns to become as familiar to you as they were to Jeremiah or Jesus or Paul, and the readings assigned for each day from the Old and New Testament will give you immediate entry to all the principal biblical narratives. For a helpful commentary on the Daily Office readings, see Joseph P. Russell's four-book series *The Daily Lectionary* (Forward Movement).

For reading and meditating on the Sunday lections, see Joseph P. Russell's *The New Prayer Book Guide to Christian Education* (Cowley, 1996), which highlights the themes of Scripture in the Sunday readings and links them to the church year season by season.

∼ Praying with Scripture

For less systematic ways of incorporating regular Bible-reading into the life of prayer while at the same time increasing your level of biblical literacy, some helpful guides are Walter Brueggemann, *Praying the Psalms* (Saint Mary's Press, 1993); Thomas Merton , *Bread in the Wilderness* (Liturgical Press, 1986); Martin L. Smith, *The Word is*

Very Near You: A Guide to Praying with Scripture (Cowley, 1989); Norvene Vest, *Bible Reading for Spiritual Growth* (Upper Room, 1996) and *No Moment Too Small: Rhythms of Silence, Prayer, and Holy Reading* (Cowley, 1992); and Linda L. Grenz, *In Dialogue with Scripture* (The Episcopal Church Center, 1993).

〜 Translations of the Bible

On the theory and history of translating the Bible, there are excellent introductory articles in *The Anchor Bible Dictionary* and *The Oxford Companion to the Bible*. See also Everett Fox's introduction to his translation of *The Five Books of Moses* (Schocken, 1995).

Three translations of portions of the Hebrew Bible in recent years have made once-familiar texts seem at once fresh, foreign, and new: David Rosenberg, *The Book of J* (Grove Weidenfeld, 1990); Fox's *The Five Books of Moses;* and Robert Alter, *Genesis* (Norton, 1996). Richmond Lattimore, long renowned for his translations of Homer and the Greek dramatists, has now collected his various translations of the New Testament writings into one volume, *The New Testament* (North Point Press/Farrar, Straus, Giroux, 1996). Stimulating new translations of two of the gospels (followed by a "gospel" of his own) are available from the distinguished novelist and critic Reynolds Price in *Three Gospels* (Scribner, 1996).

The most readily accessible and useful edition of the Nag Hammadi texts, now available in paperback, is Bentley Layton, ed., *The Gnostic Scriptures* (Anchor Books, 1995). Layton's editions and commentaries are the best available in English.

～ Midrash and Allegory

There is a wealth of accessible material on midrash and allegory. See Michael Fishbane's eloquent and challenging essays in *The Garments of Torah: Essays in Biblical Hermeneutics* (Indiana, 1992), as well as his *Biblical Interpretation in Ancient Israel* (Clarendon, 1985). On this tremendously complex topic, a good place to start is the entry on the history of interpretation in the *Oxford Companion*, particularly the sections on "Jewish Interpretation" and "Early Christian Interpretation." The entries in *The Anchor Bible Dictionary* are equally helpful, and more complete. Another place to start is the volume written jointly by James L. Kugel and Rowan A. Greer: *Early Biblical Interpretation* (Westminster, 1986).

Several accessible essays on midrash for the beginner are James L. Kugel, "Two Introductions to Midrash" and Frank Kermode, "The Plain Sense of Things," in Geoffrey H. Hartman and Sandford Budick, eds., *Midrash and Literature* (Yale, 1986); and Gerald L. Bruns, "Midrash and Allegory," in Robert Alter and Frank Kermode, *The Literary Guide to the Bible* (Harvard University Press, 1987). On Paul as an interpreter of the Hebrew Bible, two books by Jewish scholars are changing the face of Pauline studies: Daniel Boyarin, *A Radical Jew: Paul and the Politics of Identity* (Berkeley, 1994), and Alan F. Segal, *Paul the Convert: The Apostolate and Apostasy of Saul the Pharisee* (Yale, 1990).

～ History of the Bible

On the layout and meaning of the Talmud page, see the first volume of the beautiful and authoritative teaching edition of the Talmud in English by Rabbi Adin Steinsaltz, *The Talmud—The Steinsaltz Edition: A Reference Guide* (Random House, 1989), especially pages 48-59.

Some helpful treatments of the history of scroll and codex can be found in *The Cambridge History of the Bible* (Cambridge University Press, 1970). An extensive collection of photographic plates of exemplary Bible pages, along with full descriptive captions, can be found in David Norton's *A History of the Bible as Literature* (Cambridge University Press, 1993).

The best introduction to the *Glossa* and to the reading of Scripture in the Middle Ages is Beryl Smalley, *The Study of the Bible in the Middle Ages* (Basil Blackwell, 1952). For the allegorical method of reading the Bible, see the classic study by A. C. Charity, *Events and their Afterlife: The Dialectics of Christian Typology in the Bible and Dante* (Cambridge University Press, 1966), and the fine book by Dom Jean Leclercq, *The Love of Learning and the Desire for God* (Fordham, 1961).

Excellent new biographies of two of the leading figures in the history of the English Bible have just appeared: David Daniell's *William Tyndale: A Biography* (Yale, 1994), and Diarmaid MacCulloch's *Thomas Cranmer* (Yale, 1996). On the later history of the Bible in England, see Christopher Hill's *The English Bible and the Seventeenth-Century Revolution* (Allen Lane, 1993).

～ The Historical Jesus

In recent years, the work of the Jesus Seminar in California has been much in the news. One of the Seminar's more thoughtful and responsible participants is Marcus Borg, author of *Meeting Jesus Again for the First Time: The Historical Jesus and the Heart of Contemporary Faith* (HarperSanFrancisco, 1994). For a scathing critique of the Jesus Seminar, see Luke Timothy Johnson, *The Real Jesus* (HarperSanFrancisco, 1996).

Two recent "biographies" of Jesus illustrate distinct but complementary approaches to what has been called the "new quest" for the historical Jesus: John Dominic Crossan, *The Historical Jesus: The Life of a Mediterranean Jewish Peasant* (HarperSanFrancisco, 1992), and John P. Meier, *A Marginal Jew: Rethinking the Historical Jesus* (two volumes; Doubleday, 1991, 1995).

∾ Feminist Scholarship

For feminist approaches to the New Testament, a good place to start is *The Women's Bible Commentary*, Carol A. Newsom and Sharon H. Ringe, eds. (SPCK and Westminster/John Knox Press, 1992). The classic work remains Elisabeth Schüessler-Fiorenza, *In Memory of Her: A Feminist Theological Reconstruction of Christian Origins* (Crossroad, 1983). For a summary of contemporary feminist approaches, and an excellent example of one, see Janice Capel Anderson, "Feminist Criticism: The Dancing Daughter," in Janice Capel Anderson and Stephen D. Moore, *Mark and Method: New Approaches in Biblical Studies* (Fortress, 1992), pages 103-134. Anderson provides a brief and helpfully annotated bibliography.

∾ Scripture and the Episcopal Church

An illuminating example of the current debate in the Episcopal Church on the authority of the Bible can be found in the contrasting papers presented by two theologians before the Episcopal House of Bishops in 1992: Charles P. Price, "Holy Book, Holy People: A Study of the Authority and Use of the Bible," and Stephen Noll, "Reading the Bible as the Word of God," both in Frederick Houk Borsch, ed., *The Bible's Authority in Today's Church: Papers on the Authority of Scripture Presented to the Episcopal House of Bishops* (Trinity Press International, 1993). See also L. William

Countryman's *Biblical Authority or Biblical Tyranny?* (Trinity Press International and Cowley, 1994). On conversation as a model for the reading of Scripture, see Richard Norris, "The Scriptures in the Life of the Church," in Borsch, *The Bible's Authority in Today's Church.*

Finally, for eloquent sermons by an Episcopal preacher that reveal the close relationship of informed Bible reading to a baptized imagination, see Barbara Brown Taylor, *The Preaching Life* (Cowley, 1993), *Gospel Medicine* (Cowley, 1995), and *Bread of Angels* (Cowley, 1997).

∼ Audiovisual Resources

A wide variety of videotapes are available to supplement any study of the history and text of the Bible. Videotapes that might be useful in conjunction with this book include:

- a survey of the history of the Bible, including an exploration of the Holy Land and the cultures of ancient Israel;
- Scripture as the telling of stories;
- how the books of the Bible were formed and translated; and
- dramatic readings of the gospels, particularly Mark.

In Dialogue With Scripture (available from the Episcopal Church Center) provides an up-to-date, comprehensive list of audiovisuals from a number of sources. You may also contact The Episcopal Radio/TV Foundation (404-633-7800) and the Center for the Ministry of Teaching at Virginia Theological Seminary (3737 Seminary Road, Alexandria, VA 22304) directly for their lists of videotapes currently available for purchase or rental.

Questions for Group Discussion

This book may be used for a six-session introductory study of the Bible, reading one chapter before each meeting. Responses to the questions sometimes requires individual preparation prior to the class, so questions need to be read along with the chapters. These questions may be used in large or small groups, though you may find some are more fruitfully discussed in pairs or groups of three.

∼ Chapter 1

1. What are your earliest memories of reading the Bible? What did that Bible look like? How did it feel? Describe a memorable experience you once had of reading the Bible, or of hearing it read. What specific thoughts or feelings about the Bible does the memory produce for you? Do you think of the Bible any differently now?

2. Which of the following definitions matches more closely your present view of the Bible?
   - It is God's Word, written down.
   - It is an interpretation of God's dealings with humanity.

- It is a collection of ancient documents that have provided the foundation for Jewish and later for Christian believing.

How did you come to the position you now hold? What are the implications of your position for the way you read the Bible? How has your understanding of these matters changed over time? Why?

〜 Chapter 2

1. Go to your local public or parish library, or to a well-stocked bookstore, and try to find two or three different annotated versions of the Bible (for example, the *New Oxford Annotated Bible*; the *Harper/Collins Study Bible*; the *New Jerusalem Bible*; the *NIV Study Bible*). Look up the text, text notes, and annotations for several different Bible verses (perhaps Genesis 1:1, or John 3:16). Compare them. Then compare the supplementary apparatus in each edition—maps, tables of contents, indexes, appendices. How do the Bibles differ? How are they similar? Do the annotations on identical passages agree on every point? Which would you decide to purchase? Why?

2. Think of a book besides the Bible that has had a shaping influence on your life—using Walter Benjamin's word, a book that has possessed an "aura" for you. How did you come to be acquainted with it? Did someone introduce you to it, teach it to you, or interpret it? In what situation did you first read it? Have you reread the book over the years? Does it arouse the same feelings in you now as it did when you first read it?

How does the kind of experience you have had with such a book compare with the experience you have had with the Bible?

∾ Chapter 3

1. Set apart an hour or so to read the gospel of Mark without reference to chapters, verses, printed columns, annotations, or any of the other trappings of the printed Bible page. You can do this by reading it in the versions translated by Reynolds Price or Richmond Lattimore, or by listening to a recording of the gospel on tape, or by reading it aloud to yourself or having it read to you. What is important is to hear the gospel whole from start to finish as a single story.

When you have finished reading, write down your impressions. What was the experience like? What do you remember most about the story in the telling of it? What incidents or images or turns of phrase remain with you most vividly? What words would you choose to characterize Mark as a storyteller? What other parts of the Bible do you think it would be helpful to experience in the same way?

2. During the week, think of a story about yourself or your family that has been important to you over the years. In your study group, divide into pairs and let one person tell his or her story. Wait a few moments, and then have the listener tell the story back. Then reflect together on the following questions:

- Why did you tell the story the way you did? Was it the way you had heard the story originally, or had you changed it?
- Did you decide on the order of events before you started? Were all the facts accurate? How do you know? Did your story have a beginning, a middle, and an end?

- Did your listener repeat the story to you as you told it, or were changes made? If so, what were they? Why were they made?
- What might this experience reveal about the way the gospel-writers heard and told stories about Jesus?

3. Here is the way the gospel of Thomas, one of the documents discovered in the desert near the Egyptian town of Nag Hammadi in the late 1940s, tells Jesus' parable of the Great Supper:

> Jesus said, "A man had received visitors. And when he had prepared the dinner, he sent his servant to invite the guests. He went to the first one and said to him, 'My master invites you.' He said, 'I have claims against some merchants. They are coming to me this evening. I must go and give them my orders. I ask to be excused from the dinner.' He went to another and said to him, 'My master has invited you.' He said to him, 'I have just bought a house and am required for the day. I shall not have any spare time.' He went to another and said to him, 'My master invites you.' He said to him, 'My friend is going to get married, and I am to prepare the banquet. I shall not be able to come. I ask to be excused from the dinner.' He went to another and said to him, 'My master invites you.' He said to him, 'I have just bought a farm, and I am on my way to collect the rent, I shall not be able to come. I ask to be excused.'
>
> "The servant returned and said to the master, 'Those whom you invited to the dinner have asked to be excused.' The master said to his servant, 'Go outside to the streets and bring back those whom you happen to meet, so that they may dine.' Businessmen and merchants will not enter the Places of my Father." (*The Nag*

Hammadi Library in English, ed. James M. Robinson [Harper and Row, 1977].)

Read both versions of the same parable in Matthew 22 and Luke 14. How are the three stories similar? How do they differ? Could the Thomas version have been closer to the original? How might someone tell?

4. Read the two accounts of creation found in Genesis. The first account (Genesis 1:1–2:4) has been thought by scholars to be a product of the Priestly tradition, while the second account (Genesis 2:5-24) is thought to be part of the J or Yahwistic tradition. Comparing the two versions, what kinds of differences do you read or hear in style, tone, or content? Do you prefer one version to the other? Why? Why do you suppose the canon finally included both?

∽ **Chapter 4**

1. Compare these two readings of 1 Corinthians 7:21:

Were you a slave when called? Do not be concerned about it. Even if you gain your freedom, make use of your present condition now more than ever. (NOAB)

Were you a slave when you were called? Do not let that trouble you; but if a chance of liberty should come, take it. (REB)

These are two different translations of the same text. What do you make of them? What does each version imply about Paul and his support of slavery? How would we decide which version is more accurate? What might be at stake for us in deciding what Paul actually wrote?

2. Consider this excerpt from the prologue of John's gospel, taken from a recently published inclusive version of the New Testament:

> And the Word became flesh and lived among us, and we have seen the Word's glory, the glory as of a parent's only child [or the only Child of the Father-Mother], full of grace and truth. (John testified to the child and cried out, "This was the one of whom I said, 'The one who comes after me ranks ahead of me because that one was before me.'") From the fullness of the Child we have all received, grace upon grace. The law indeed was given through Moses; grace and truth came through Jesus Christ. No one has ever seen God. It is God the only Child, who is close to the bosom of the Father-Mother, who has made God known. (*The New Testament and Psalms: An Inclusive Version* [Oxford, 1996].)

Compare this passage to the *New Revised Standard* translation of John 1:14-18. You might also want to review the principles on which the new version is based, as outlined in chapter 4. Why did the editors of the inclusive version change the wording of the NRSV? In the new version, what has been gained? What has been lost?

∾ Chapter 5

1. In the NOAB or a similar study Bible, look up Matthew 5:31-32, where Jesus condemns divorce. Trace the cross-references provided. What light do they shed on Jesus' strong statements? What authority do these passages have for us today? Is the church wrong to allow divorced persons to remarry?

2. Two notoriously difficult passages in the Bible are Genesis 15:7-21 and 1 Corinthians 8:1-13. The first describes a

mysterious covenant ceremony conducted between Yahweh and Abraham, and the second concerns Paul's opinions
about the Corinthian practice of eating meat sacrificed to
idols. What help do your Bible's explanatory notes offer
you as you try to understand these passages? Are there
questions they do not answer? Where would you go next?

⤳ **Chapter 6**

1. During the week read Psalm 126, using the notes provided in an annotated Bible. Spend time each day memorizing the psalm by praying it aloud, using the NRSV
translation. When you gather as a group, say the psalm
together, this time antiphonally, with half the group saying
the odd-numbered verses, and the other half of the group
responding with the even-numbered verses. Again, try to
do this all from memory.

Now reflect together on the experience. How easy or
difficult was it for you to memorize the psalm? What did
the psalm mean to you when you first began to memorize
it? What did it mean to you after a week of repetition? Did
the experience of reciting it in a group differ from the
experience of reciting it individually? If so, how and why?
What is the difference between a silent reading of the psalm
and this oral experience of _ruminatio?_

2. Many parish churches follow the ancient custom of
performing a dramatic reading of the Passion narrative at
the Palm Sunday and Good Friday liturgies, with different
people taking on the various speaking parts, and the congregation taking the part of the crowd. What makes this
experience different from a silent reading of the story? Does
this kind of performance affect the meaning of the narrative? What happens to our experience of the story when
readers become participants in the action?

C owley Publications is a ministry of the Society of St. John the Evangelist, a religious community for men in the Episcopal Church. Emerging from the Society's tradition of prayer, theological reflection, and diversity of mission, the press is centered in the rich heritage of the Anglican Communion.

Cowley Publications seeks to provide books, audio cassettes, and other resources for the ongoing theological exploration and spiritual development of the Episcopal Church and others in the body of Christ. To this end, it is dedicated to developing a new generation of theological writers, encouraging them to produce timely, creative, and stimulating publications of excellence, and making these publications available widely, reaching both clergy and lay persons.